Australian Prayers & Psalms

PART I

Australian Psalms

PART II

Australian Prayers

PART III

Never Alone

Bruce D. Prewer

Ideas into Books: WESTVIEW®
Kingston Springs, Tennessee, USA

Ideas into Books: Westview®
P.O. Box 605
Kingston Springs, TN 37082 USA
www.ideasintobooks.net

ISBN: 978-1-62880-145-3

Second Edition, July 2018

Digitally Printed on acid-free paper.

PART I

Australian Psalms

Australian Psalms

has been reproduced
from the 12th printing of the
1984 Lutheran Publishing House Edition.

Contents

Part I: The Sound of Joy

Everything That Draws Breath . . 10
Reflection of the Unseen 12
Grace of Our Lord Jesus Christ . 13
Australian Accent 14
Jesus 16
Morning Sunlight 18
Happiness 19
The Ways of God 20
Familiar Things 22
Exuberant Praise 23
The Bountiful God 24
Joys of Home Life 26
A New Song 27
Faith, Hope, and Love 28
Christians Together 29

Slighty Less than Gods 30
For Things That Go Well . . 31
His Works around Us 32
Never Alone 34
The Wind 35
Father of the Lights 36
Astounding God 37
Worship in a Caravan Park . 38
The Voice of God 39
Our City 40
Baptism 42
Holy Communion 43
The Divine Secret 44
Who Am I? 46
Jesus Is King 48

Part II: The Shame and the Glory

Holiness 50
Penitence 52
How Long? 53
Rebellion 54
Homes 55
The Still Centre 56
The Only Hope 57
When We Are Feeling Down . . 58
Healing 59
His Arms 60
Our Work 62
Happy People 63

The Body 64
Brother 65
God's Strength 66
When 67
This Mystery 68
Judgment 70
Dependable Word 71
God Hidden and Present . . 72
Hunger and Thirst 74
Forsaken? 76
Sweet and Sour 78

continued . . .

Part III: These Are the Days

Come, Lord Jesus 80
The Word within the Word . .82
Prepare the Way of the Lord .84
He Comes 87
The Leap Forward 88
On Christmas Eve 90
Christmas 92
That Day 93
For the New Year 94
Epiphany 96
The Way of the Cross 98
Following in His Ways 99
Not by Bread Alone 100
For the Affluent 102
Don't Tempt God 103
Don't Test God 104
One Lord 106

God Alone 108
The Lost 110
From the Depths 111
Hosanna 112
Good Friday 114
Easter 115
Pentecost 116
Life in the Spirit 118
Our God 119
All Saints' Day 120
Australia Day 122
Anzac Day 124
Church Anniversary 125
Come Quickly! 126

Photo Credits 128

To my
best friend:
Marie

Introduction

Until we discover God at work here in Australia, in the secular as well as the religious events, the Australian Church will not find itself and its destiny.

We 'down under' are oppressed by an insidious inferiority complex which makes us believe that the real events happen only on the other side of the world. We tend to think that the 'really real' things happened (and still happen) in Israel, Britain, and Europe; even in the USA a few real things occur! Everything in Australia seems 'less real' and therefore can't be taken as seriously. Our culture and our Christian sub-culture are dependent on the northern, largely-European scene. Theirs is the only real history; nothing ever really started to happen in Australia until Europeans came 200 years ago. Even the geography seems 'less real'; Ben Lomond or Mt Carmel, the fields of Devon, and the Rhine Valley seem 'more real' than Kosciusko or Cradle Mountain, the paddocks at Kingaroy, and the Derwent Valley.

If we are to throw off this cultural self-deprecation, we must see the Creator still at work here in Australia, as he has been from the beginning. But we won't see this until we begin to accept the Aboriginal culture and history as an authentic part of our history. We will not find ourselves until we humbly discover them as a profound part of the 'really real'.

The psalms in this book are a tiny, timid attempt to take God's Australia seriously in geographic terms. But they fail abysmally in historical terms because, to my shame, I am largely ignorant of the Aboriginal heritage. Perhaps the authentic Australian psalms will be written by our Aboriginals. Perhaps they are already composed, but our ears are switched off.

In this collection, in addition to my original psalms, there are a number of transpositions of biblical psalms. These are not translations. By 'transpositions' I mean that the setting is transposed from Israel to Australia, and from BC to AD times. For this reason, these psalms should not be read as a substitute for sound Bible translations. Nevertheless they are offered as material for worship, both public and private, just as they arose out of worship, both public and private.

Bruce Prewer,
March 1979

PART I
The Sound of Joy

Everything That Draws Breath

God, our wonderful God, you make everything that delights
        the eye;
    Yours is the gift of everything that draws breath.

Yours is the energy that vibrates the wing of a bee,
    The gracefulness of black swans skimming over still lakes,
The joy of a puppy bounding to greet its owner,
    The courage of a shelduck leading ducklings to safe waters,
The song of a magpie on a soft spring morning,
    The beauty of pink galahs wheeling over trees at sunset,
The purpose in mutton birds returning to southern sand-hills,
    The warmth surrounding the joey in a kangaroo's pouch.

Yours, Creator God, is the skill of the wedge-tailed eagle,
    The play of the bandicoot on warm summer nights,
The strength of the baby koala clinging to its mother,
    The authority of seagulls riding salty winds,
The games of the dolphin surfing among swimmers,
    The communal chatter of colourful parrots,
The vigour of the trout leaping in quiet waters,
    The persistence of fairy penguins waddling up sandy slopes.

Yours, wonderful God, is the dance of the slender brolga,
    The industry of the ant through long summer days,
The power of the buffalo breaking through thickets,
    The glory on the radiant wings of a beetle,
The excitement of the platypus hunting for yabbies,
    The agility of mountain minnows darting between shaded rocks,
The wariness of the wallaby peeping from among bushes,
    The confidence of the sparrow winning crusts from pigeons.

Yours, Lord, truly yours, is the laughter of the kookaburra,
  The speed of an emu striding through mallee scrub,
The comedy of the crab side-scurrying over wet sand,
  The searching of the cockatoo for a place to nest,
The effortless padding of a dingo over saltbush plains,
  The conversation of the blackbirds at early morning,
The vision of the wombat as it rummages through long dark nights,
  The display of the lyre bird as he shares in creation's joy.

God, our wonderful God, you make everything that delights
    the eye;
  Yours is the gift of everything that draws breath!

Seals at Seal Bay, South Australia.

Reflection of the Unseen

Colossians 1

At the time when shadows were around us
and fears choked our joy,
You, most wonderful God, transferred us
into the kingdom of the Son of Love,
where there is the light
and liberty of the children of God.

Like the reflection of the sunrise
beaming over placid waters,
so is our Lord the true reflection
of you, our unseen God;
the beginning of all that was,
and the joyous completion
of all that is to be.

Our little planet
and the vast worlds in outer space
were spun by his power!
The things we see and discover,
and things no eye has seen
nor mind comprehended,
are all subject to his power
and filled with his purpose.

His ways are before all other.
The grace that coheres all things
is his and his alone.
The Church is his making
and he is its only head,
the first risen from all death,
the only Son to be named Lord.

Wonderful is your choice,
Most loving God,
to make the fullness of your nature
dwell in our True-Man Jesus,

reconciling the whole cosmos
to yourself through him,
bringing gracious peace
through that most bloody cross;
peace in time and eternity
through him alone.

Grace of Our Lord Jesus Christ

How shall we ever praise our Lord enough,
    Or serve him as he surely deserves?
His grace moves faster than light;
    His mercy is larger than the universe.

In every part of our home planet,
    Grace works without limit.
It saturates the weary centuries
    And fully fills each minute.

No nation is denied his grace
    Nor is any child outside it.
The cities and the farms partake alike;
    It works in lives that still deride it.

So deep that none can fall beneath it;
    In all the world no one is missed.
Our sins rise up, but ever higher
    His grace will rise and still persist.

What God's grace launched in Christ,
    Will one day be completed.
And though it suffer from a million blows,
    His grace will never be depleted.

Australian Accent

Brother, does the dust of Australia cling to your feet,
      as did the dust of Palestine?
Is your skin tanned like a jackeroo,
      and do you tend wounds in bush nursing hospitals?
Has Galilee become Lake St Clair or Jindabyne,
      and do fishermen still ferry you in their boats?

Brother, do you watch the crimson face of the waratah open,
      as you watched the lilies of the field?
Are you teaching us lessons from the kookaburra
      as you did from sparrows and ravens?
Do the wallaby and platypus delight you,
      providing a thought for an unforgettable text?

Brother, has Jericho moved to Alice Springs,
      and does Zacchaeus meet you under the river gums?
Have you walked through the wheatfields of the Mallee,
      or harvested with farmers at Parkes and Ceduna?
Do you tell stories to the cane workers at Bundaberg,
      or create parables from Barossa vineyards?

Brother, do you choose friends among the girls of Kings Cross,
      or make disciples from the drug-pushers of St Kilda?
When black people hold a wedding celebration,
      do you join them in corroboree?
When our migrant neighbours are abused,
      will you tell us the 'Parable of the Good Italian'?

Brother, what money-tables anger you today;
      are our cathedrals and churches dens of thieves?
Do Pilate and Herod still misgovern us,
      and are Australian crowds easily bought for Barabbas?
Do Pharisees or Sadducees now wear clerical collars,
      and does Caiaphas lobby for favours at Canberra?

Brother, do you pray at night in our bushland,
   or weep in the Gethsemane of our city parks?
Are you now betrayed by an Australian Judas,
   and deserted by your closest mates?
Have men become Peter and denied you
   in universities, pubs, and RSL clubs?

Brother, is the cross now made of scribbly gum,
   and do the nails come from BHP?
Are you lifted up outside our cities
   and is Golgotha near every country town?

When you pray forgiveness on us all,
   isn't it an Australian accent that we hear?

Outback signposts, Queensland.

Jesus

Jesus, Son of Man,
   Jesus, Son of God,
radiance of the Father,
   first-born among many brothers:
to you belongs our sole allegiance
   and our everlasting gratitude!

When our world was ripe
   for despair or faith,
   you came to us.
With our uprooted hopes
lying fruitless around us,
   you shared our dust
   and planted a true vine
which shall ever be fruitful.

While proud and cultured men
   chased philosophical fashions,
   or created scribal absurdities,
You told unforgettable parables
   about farmers, servants, and wedding parties,
seeding the furrows of history
   with a potent Word bearing a harvest
   too vast for all the silos of this world.

In the terrible time of your dereliction,
when man attained his worst hour,
   you hung on that awful Cross
   bearing on tortured shoulders
   the sins of the whole world,
till in the gathering darkness
   you knew the task was done
   and the reconciliation begun.

In the light of Easter dawn,
    while disciples in whispers
    passed their despair one to another,
You arose at the call of the Father,
bringing light and immortality to light,
    warming hearts with inextinguishable joy,
    and rehabilitating doubters and deniers
with a love that overpowers the gates of hell.

Jesus, the Word made flesh,
    Jesus, friend of sinners,
Reconciler of the whole universe,
    the resurrection and the life:
Heaven and earth are full of your glory!
Our allegiance and gratitude are yours for ever!

Morning Sunlight

As the morning sun falls on tiled roof-tops
  and spreads warmth in east-west alleys,
My whole being rises to give praise;
  my every fibre rejoices in God.

Cars speeding on the freeway sparkle in light;
  in sunshine even the buses seem young again.
Already builders are at work on new houses,
  perched on rafters soaked with sunlight.
Laughing children skip their way to schoolgrounds,
  or pedal small bikes with spokes aflashing.
Across parks people short-cut to work —
  ladies stilt-stepping and men strong-striding.
Little children sun-dance to kinder,
  escorted by mothers, sisters, and brothers.
An old lady potters in her front garden;
  her husband promises the terrier a walk.
Overhead, gleaming planes jet interstate,
  while their teachers, the starlings, gather on power-lines.

Fruitcart, Rundle Mall, Adelaide.

Trains hoot through suburban crossings,
    and delivery vans begin their bustle.
Everything has wakened at the old sun's bidding;
    our whole city embraces a bright new day.

Blessed be your name, Giver of sunlight.
    Blessed be your name, Author of life.
Glory be to you, Lord of our city.
    Glory be to you, Renewer of life.

Happiness

Psalm 1

Happiness is the person who shuns unloving ways,
    who is not attracted by apathy or sarcasm,
But finds delight in Jesus' teaching,
    testing it out by day and by night.

Such people are like great red gums
    growing by the riverside;
Flowering every season, defying drought,
    and constantly putting forth new growth.

Not so unloving people;
    they are like grass in a willy-willy.
When pressure is on they can't take it,
    nor can they stand the company of good folk.

Those who love have their tap-roots in God;
    the unloving are rootless.
The Lord can work with loving people,
    but the unloving work their own ruin.

The Ways of God

Psalm 19

The Southern Cross signals God's glory;
    the Milky Way gleams with his handiwork.
Every new day tells his story;
    at night-time his skills are displayed.
All nations and tongues can understand his language;
    his message saturates our planet.
Look at the merry old sun in his robes of light;
    he smiles like a bridegroom on his wedding day.
Keen as an athlete at the Olympics,
    he strides from Sydney to Perth.
Then he sprints the other half of the circuit,
    missing no nation with his warmth.

How complete are the ways of the Lord,
    constantly restoring our humanity.
He is a dependable counsellor,
    with wisdom for those who have open minds.
The Lord's purposes are beautiful,
    making our heart leap with joy.
His commands are clear,
    bringing a new light into our eyes.
The respect he arouses is healthy,
    extending for ever.
His assessment of us is fair,
    completely to be trusted.
His word is more valuable than a fortune,
    more precious than reserves of gold.
It is sweeter than the finest confectionery,
    more natural than the honey of mallee blossom.
It keeps your servants alert and sensitive;
    living by it brings us incomparable gain.

If we should think he has made mistakes,
    it's time to check our own motives.
Save your servants from self-conceit,
    from the deadly reign of ego.

Then shall we live without shame,
    free from the worst of all treason.
May these words tumbling from the mouth,
    and the feelings surging in the heart,
Be acceptable in your eyes,
    dear Lord, our true strength and our Saviour.

Familiar Things

Sing from the mountain-tops and shout to the skies!
   Praise him all his messengers, and cheer him all his servants!
Let the whole of our continent praise the Lord:
   mountain and desert, river, waterfall, and farmland.
Let the vegetation praise the Lord:
   gum tree and wattle, blackboys, boronia, and lotus lily.
Let all animals praise the Lord:
   koala and kangaroo, Tasmanian devil, possum, and wombat.
Let the birds of plain and forest praise the Lord:
   galah and emu, blue wren, honeyeater, and jabiru.
Let coastland and seas praise the Lord:
   surf and tides, beaches, coral, and rock-pool.
Let everything in the seas praise the Lord:
   seal and penguin, starfish, snapper, and dolphin.
Let our cities take time to praise the Lord:
   park and street, housewife, garbage-man, and councillor.
Let all music praise the Lord:
   guitar and organ, orchestra, pop-group, and didgeridoo.
Let everything living under the sun,
   everything that is or ever will be,
   praise the Lord! Hallelujah!

Brushtailed possums, Queensland.

Exuberant Praise

Psalm 148

Cheer the Lord, everyone!
   Everything, praise him!

Cheer him from our skies;
   praise him from outer space.
Cheer him, you astronauts;
   praise him, all children of the stars.
Cheer him, sun and moon;
   praise him, all distant galaxies.
Cheer him, all who are close to his heart;
   praise him, all mysteries beyond our knowledge.
All of you, cheer the Lord,
   for he speaks and you come into being.
He gives you a place for ever;
   He fixes the universal laws.

Cheer the Lord from this planet earth:
   rolling ocean and powerful hurricane;
Lightning, hail, snow, and ice;
   wind and storm fulfilling his purposes;
Our mountains, plains, and hills;
   our orchards, cane-fields, and forests;
Kangaroo, possum, and platypus;
   lizard and snake, black swan and rosella parrot.

Prime ministers and presidents of the earth;
   Cabinet ministers and high court judges;
Exuberant teenagers,
   old people and children,
Come on, all of you, cheer the Lord;
   he alone is worth it!
His glory transfigures this earth,
   and blazes from a million suns.
He has given mankind high honour;
   heroes will applaud his faithfulness.
Those who trust his presence will shout:
   'Cheer the Lord!'

The Bountiful God

Psalm 104

With all my being I celebrate the Lord!
  My wonderful God, you are dressed in glorious love!
You come to us as bright as the sunlight,
  and signal to us out of the star-flecked sky.
You refresh us with rain and play on tumbling clouds,
  and ride on the wings of the wind.
The breezes are your messengers,
  and the sparkling fire is your servant.

In the first travail of our planet's birth,
  while earth's crust settled and seas found their shores,
While mountains stood tall and valleys nestled below,
  you were present with a word insistent as thunder.
You were the one who first poured streams down valleys,
  letting the kangaroo drink and the cockatoo quench his thirst.
You saw the kookaburra settle in the scrub,
  laughing from among the branches,
While the mountain ash lifted high its head,
  and the river gums gave nesting place to the owl and parrot.

Even now you are still at work;
  on the rocky hills you shelter the wallaby and lizard.
The farmers look up as the clouds still give sweet rain,
  so that the grass grows and the sheep and cattle are fed.
Over the wheat crops the showers spread,
  the thirsty vineyards are watered;
On the slopes the banana plantations are refreshed,
  till the face of man shines with happiness.

Your sun and moon revolve on,
  regulating all waking and sleeping;
After dark the wild creatures are on the move,
  then at dawn they slink back to their lairs.
In the rhythm of this good life man gets up to work;
  tired, he comes home at night and receives rest.

Lord, everything you do is so bountiful!
   The wide sea swarms with tuna, prawns, and mackerel.
The world teems with living things, all depending on you,
   taking what you offer, feeding from your hands.
If you should hide your face, fear would overtake us;
   if you should withdraw your breath, all would be no more.
But you would only have to speak and all would be renewed;
   the face of the earth would be radiant again.

May your rule last for ever!
   May you always find joy in your precious planet!
We tremble with joy at your glance!
   We come to life at your touch!

Wheatfields, Western Australia.

Joys of Home Life

Let us praise the Lord for his goodness:

For our homes of the past and homes of today,
precious memories and present joys.
   Hallelujah, hallelujah!

For the intimate fun of family celebrations,
the enrichment of guests at our family meal.
   Hallelujah, hallelujah!

For the cries and cooing of a first baby,
the thrill of watching a child become adult.
   Hallelujah, hallelujah!

For little people chatting with make-believe presences,
and dolls, scooters, finger-paintings, and birthdays.
   Hallelujah, hallelujah!

For pets that make our home their own —
dogs, guinea-pigs, cats, and budgies.
   Hallelujah, hallelujah!

For familiar walls holding out a storm,
and chairs and beds which have 'our feel' about them.
   Hallelujah, hallelujah!

For the shared excitement of planning things new,
and sorrowing together when things go wrong.
   Hallelujah, hallelujah!

For the love which allows us to be irritable with each other,
weakness accepted and strengths shared.
   Hallelujah, hallelujah!

For fragile ties which hold under strain,
forgiveness sought and forgiveness given.
   Hallelujah, hallelujah!

For our homes of today and homes yet to come,
present joys and hopes for tomorrow,
   Hallelujah, hallelujah, hallelujah!

A New Song

Psalm 98

Come, sing a new song to God,
   for he has worked wonders!

With the strength of redeeming love
   he is saving creation.
He has brought his actions into the open,
   showing his love to all nations.
He has not forgotten his servants of old
   to whom he was so loyal;
But now every country on earth
   shall see what our God is doing.

Join the celebrations everyone,
   shout and sing for joy!
Praise God with the guitar;
   add your voice to the strings.
Join in with trumpet and drums
   till a joyful noise greets our King.
Let the sea roar and everything in it,
   the land and everything on it.
Come on, rivers, clap your hands,
   and you mountains, join the choir!

For the Lord comes to govern our planet,
   to deal out a new kind of justice,
And to make mercy his rule.

Faith, Hope, and Love

Faith like a mustard seed,
Power so small:
Word growing into deed,
Reaching tall,
Gift for all.

Hope making all things new,
Vision grand:
Christ's dream which shall come true,
In our land,
Near at hand.

Love larger than the world,
Christ's new song:
Power from which death recoiled,
Love so strong,
We belong.

Faith, hope, and love are free,
Boundless store;
New heaven and earth shall be
Without flaw,
Evermore.

This may be sung to the opening horn call from Schubert's Symphony in C, 'The Gre

Christians Together

Give praise to God who joins us here,
Whose healing Spirit casts out fear:
    Hallelujah, hallelujah!
Let each our neighbour's joy partake,
And to our God thanksgiving make.
    O praise him, O praise him,
    Hallelujah, hallelujah, hallelujah!

Give praise to God who gives us Christ,
Whose love redeems a mighty host:
    Hallelujah, hallelujah!
Let each our neighbour's faith uphold,
And to our God our joy be told.
    O praise him, O praise him,
    Hallelujah, hallelujah, hallelujah!

Give praise to God whose Spirit leads,
To serve mankind in all its needs:
    Hallelujah, hallelujah!
Let each our neighbour's hope repair,
And to our God all joy now share.
    O praise him, O praise him,
    Hallelujah, hallelujah, hallelujah!

This may be sung to the tune, *Lasst uns erfreuen*.

Slightly Less than Gods

Psalm 8

God, our God, yours is the most wonderful name in all the world,
   the highest joy in the whole universe!
Little children know this and grow strong;
   rebellious adults break themselves against your truth.
I see your fingers at work in vast galaxies;
   sun and moon obey you to the very second.
I can't help wondering why you remember mankind,
   why you bother about creatures like us.
Yet you have made us only slightly less than gods,
   trusting us with remarkable responsibility.
You have asked us to take charge of our land,
   making all other creatures subject to our authority:
The cattle and sheep, the kangaroo and crocodile,
   wedge-tailed eagle, magpie, and cockatoo,
Barramundi, tuna, dolphin, and shark,
   turtles, fairy penguins, and seals.
O God, our dear God,
   yours is the most astounding name in all the world!

Most s-w tip of Australia, Cape Leeuwin, Western Australia

For Things That Go Well

In a world where many things go wrong,
 we praise you, God, for things that go well:
Marriages that are sound and beautiful,
 each person nurtured in respect and love.
Grandparents who share the make-believe of children,
 and grandchildren who love deeply in response.
Families where there is no generation-gap,
 where members can be together or apart without fuss.

We praise you for natural things taken for granted,
 the normal rhythm of continuing creation:
Trees that purify the polluted air,
 breathing in our waste and giving us oxygen.
The robust old sun that never rests,
 encouraging up from the earth our daily bread.
The never-failing power of water to quench our thirst —
 and a dozen tasty drinks dependent on it.

We praise you, God, for national parks,
 where kangaroo will not hide from man;
For places where parrots will share our picnics,
 and kookaburras laugh from nearby trees;
Lakes which mirror sunrise and sunset,
 home for duck, ibis, and leaping fish;
Protected forests where lyre-birds still display;
 and for desert flowers, celebrating for countless years.

We praise you for folk who love their neighbours,
 genuinely looking for no reward.
For much-criticized churches which still keep going,
 treasuring the Gospel in spite of the cynics.
For the influence of that matchless Jesus,
 the best name in our prayers since childhood.
For the unearned times of courage, joy, love, and light,
 when your grace becomes our joy.

His Works around Us

Psalm 147

What joy it is to sing hymns to our God!
    Praise is a sheer delight!
The Lord is rebuilding Australia;
    he is gathering the homeless people of the world.
He heals the broken-hearted,
    and bandages their wounds.

This is the same God who knows every star;
    he has a name for each planet and moon.
Powerful beyond all imagining is he;
    no computer can process his wisdom.
This wonderful Lord lifts up the meek;
    he throws the arrogant to the ground.
Sing a hymn of thanksgiving to the Lord!
    Let all melody and harmony give praise to our God!

It is he who fills the summer sky with clouds,
    preparing rain for the parched earth.
He clothes the hills with a garment of green,
    and supplies juice in the fruit of our orchards.
On cattle stations the animals find feed,
    even wild budgerigars get their share.
In winter the fleecy snowfields are his gifts,
    and crisp frosts express his laws.
Icicles are his delicate sculpture;
    frozen lakes lie still at his bidding.
Then at his wish the ice is melted;
    the warm winds blow and the rivers flow.

The Lord is not impressed with our technology;
    nor has he pleasure in strong-arm tactics.
His pleasure is in those who respect him,
    who trust their lives to his love.
Honour the Lord, you Australians!
    Praise him from Darwin to Hobart!
For he offers new possibilities to all our people,
    and blessings on all our children.

He has given us a country at peace,
   with more food than we can eat.
His laws can be relied on in every situation;
   his Word is faster than sound.
To our pioneers he made known his Word;
   his love and justice are proclaimed in our land.

No nation has fared better than Australia —
   yet is his rule accepted in many hearts?
O sing to the Lord a new song!
   Let the whole nation praise the Lord!

Never Alone

Psalm 139

Lord, you see right through me,
　　and know me utterly.
You understand what I'm thinking,
　　long before I understand myself.
You are with me on the crowded street;
　　beside me when I go alone to bed.
Everything I do, you recognize;
　　my tongue never wags without you hearing.
I find you in my yesterdays and tomorrows,
　　your love firmly around me.
All this is too much for me;
　　It is beyond my understanding.

Where could I evade you?
　　Where could I escape your presence?
If I live high with the jet-set, you are there.
　　If I make my bed on a park bench, you are there.
If I could take off at the speed of light
　　and travel the freeways of outer space,
Even there your hand would touch me,
　　your right hand would hold me.
If I fear something awful will happen,
　　like being swallowed by darkness,
My darkness will begin to shine like the day;
　　for with you darkness becomes light.

How precious are your plans for me, Lord;
　　they add up to a fantastic number.
If I tried to count them
　　they would outnumber the sand.
Whenever I wake up to what's happening
　　I find I'm still with you!
Lord, take a hard look at me;
　　untangle my untidy motives.
Sort me out with your relentless mercy;
　　weigh up all my ideas.
Tear away whatever is unloving in me,
　　and lead me into your never-ending future.

The Wind

Like the wind swaying through mountain trees,
   Or surging through thickets of wattle,
So, Lord, is your presence with us;
   Your power thrusts through our lives.
You sweep away our petty worries
   And shake us free from fears.
At your pressure we move and sway together,
   As if we were of one mind.

Sometimes you are as strong as winter storms,
   At others as soft as the rustling of ferns.
We are taught to bend and not be broken,
   To be flexible without shifting ground.
You test the strength of our feet
   And whatever proves shallow is uprooted.

On calm days we rest content,
   Glad to watch each other in stillness;
Enjoying quietness because we know
   You are still with us.

Stand of wattles, Western Australia.

Father of the Lights

The Letter of James

Father of the lights of heaven,
God of the faith that works:
    Every good gift you present to us,
    unchanging legacies you give us.
    Not in passing moods
    but in calculated love
    you offer us a new vision
    through Jesus, Prince of light.

Father of the lights of heaven,
God of the faith that works:
    When our wisdom crumbles,
    you bring us true insight —
    uncomfortable yet comforting,
    costly yet absolutely free!
    Bonus-God, you never ignore
    or rebuff the child who asks.

Father of the lights of heaven,
God of the faith that works:
    Your brand of wisdom is practical,
    it is cheerful and merciful,
    rich in compassionate deeds
    and the foe of empty words.
    There is no longer room for blame,
    for the Lord is full of compassion.

Father of the lights of heaven,
God of the faith that works:
    Happy are those who remain true!
    Happy are the inheritors of your grace!
    They possess the promised gift,
    the large love of God,
    where widows and orphans are treasured
    more than crowns and fortunes!

Astounding God

Astounding God!
Today I want to praise you
for amazing grace:

finding without seeking . . .
possessing without keeping . . .
the end where the beginning begins . . .
good news that is offensive . . .
doubting which is believing . . .
uselessness which is most useful . . .
the word that is speechless . . .
the death which dies . . .
poverty which owns the universe . . .
memory that looks forward . . .
emptiness which overflows . . .
bread which creates hunger . . .
mystery that is unmistakable . . .
the folly which is wisdom . . .
the Cross which is glory . . .
the God who is a servant.

For amazing grace
today I want to praise you!
Astounding God!

Worship in a Caravan Park

For the sounds of this summer morning:
    call of finches in the surrounding scrub,
    incessant vibration of innumerable insects,
    flopping of thongs as a camper goes by,
    song of a magpie in a bare-limbed tree,
    rattle of breakfast dishes from caravans,
    gossip of sparrows at play in the dust,
    chatter of two children in holiday glee,
    and the background roar of the restless sea:
I thank you, Creator Spirit.

For the sights of this holiday morning:
    two grey herons on the flanks of the river,
    distant effervescence of breaking waves,
    colourful towels drying in the breeze,
    tangled-haired surfer eager for his fun,
    regiment of seagulls ranked on a spit,
    small boy carrying milk to his tent,
    rhythm of joggers on their morning run,
    and swallows glistening in the shining sun:
I thank you, Creator Spirit.

For the smells of this summer morning:
    sweet fragrance of tea-tree blossom,
    unmistakable odour of seaweed,
    aroma of toast, coffee, and tea,
    smell of salt in the wind so clean,
    fumes of oil from an outboard motor,
    scent of coconut from sunburn cream,
    and the smell of cormorants perched upstream:
I thank you, Creator Spirit.

For the feel of this holiday morning:
    bare legs warming in summer sun,
    supporting contours of a strong beach chair,
    awareness of belonging to land, sea, and sky,
    delight of breathing unpolluted air,

feel of sand between one's toes,
hand of a loved one sharing the joys,
freedom from duties and every care,
and the soft breeze caressing cheek and hair:
I thank you, Creator Spirit.

The Voice of God

Psalm 29

Give yourselves to the Lord, children of God!
    Give to the Lord all power and glory!
Offer him the praise his name deserves!
    Worship him with wholeness of life!

The voice of the Lord is stronger than rushing streams;
    above the thundering surf of the oceans he speaks.
Listen to the mighty word of the Lord;
    filled with majesty is his message.
His voice could splinter Tasmanian blue gums;
    the cedars of New England would shatter in pieces.
At his word mountains would leap like the wallaby,
    Kosciusko and the Cradle like the red kangaroo.
If the Lord commanded it, Ayers Rock would split,
    torn asunder as from fierce fire.
The voice of the Lord whips up the Gibson Desert;
    he whirls the Simpson into red dust storms.
When he speaks, forest giants are uprooted,
    or the mulga scrub is stripped bare.
Those who live close to him are in awe,
    while everything shouts 'Glory!'

From the very beginning, the Lord alone is King;
    his government is established for ever.
Lovingly he gives strength to his people;
    in his blessing is our joy and peace.

Our City

King of the City not made with hands,
    Lord of the New Jerusalem,
We thank you for our worldly city,
    We praise you for our populous home.

For office blocks and slender skyscrapers,
    And the sturdy architecture of our forebears;
For busy streets and crowded lanes,
    Government House and city squares:
        We thank you, Lord.

For lunch-hour bustle and Friday rush;
    Window-shopping when things close down;
For city arcades with little shops;
    Large emporium and shopping-town:
        We thank you, Lord.

For cricket ground and sun-browned crowd,
    Golf course, bowling alley, and hockey field;
For lovely parks, fountains, and flowers,
    Botanical gardens with trees of the world:
        We thank you, Lord.

For street-sweepers toiling while we sleep;
    Policemen untangling a traffic snarl;
For garbage collectors and their chugging trucks,
    Fire engines with sirens all awail:
        We thank you, Lord.

For water in taps, piped from the hills;
    Buses at our stop and trains at the station;
For electricity at the switch and gas in the heater;
    Evening newspapers with news of our nation:
        We thank you, Lord.

For the rich variety of films and plays,
   Visits of ballet and opera stars;
For symphony orchestras and massed choirs,
   Pop concerts and twang of guitars:
     We thank you, Lord.

For churches, Sunday-schools, and clubs,
   The vaulted cathedral with tall steeple;
For divine gifts in limitless patterns,
   And the face of Jesus in countless people:
     We thank you, Lord.

Sydney Harbour and Opera House.

Baptism

Lord, we stand awed
in the presence of your evangelist:
this tiny baby thing who dares
to be your child!

Not one word can she speak,
this your little messenger;
yet in the silence she declares
the living Word!

She has no prior faith
and brings no creed or prayer,
but from this font she bears
the faith of Christ!

She offers now no promises
nor deeds of righteousness,
but here receives and shares
the righteousness of God!

Helpless, she comes today,
carried in the arms of others,
yet in her helplessness she wears
your massive strength!

Lord, this is the greatest thing:
here a child has Brother, Friend,
and a Father who cares
world without end!

Holy Communion

I have visited Bethlehem's sacred site,
trod the worn stones of the ancient square,
from the shepherds' fields I saw the sun go down
and watched the guiding stars appear —
    but my Lord was not especially there.

In Nazareth's streets there were children at play,
and carpenters laughed as they made a repair,
the market was decked with bright garments and fruits,
while old men washed feet for their midday prayer —
    but my Lord was not especially there.

I have walked on the banks of Galilee,
listened to the waves on its pebbly shore,
seen shepherds guide flocks beside still waters,
and heard fishermen's voices on the morning air —
    but my Lord was not especially there.

On streets of Jerusalem were cascades of people,
barrows, donkeys, and porters with loads to bear;
I rejoiced on Mount Zion, in Gethsemane whispered,
and to an upper room climbed by a well-worn stair —
    but my Lord was not especially there.

In a tiny church under an Australian sun,
the farmlands shimmering with summer glare,
I've knelt with a few other ordinary souls
round a Table spread with the simplest fare —
    and truly my Lord was especially there.

The Divine Secret

Ephesians 1

To the God and Father of our Lord Jesus Christ,
    Let our honour and praise be joyfully given!
In Christ the supreme blessings of eternity
    Are lavished on the children of time and dust!

Before the creation of the universe began,
    Before our planet received its shape and colour,
When tree had not yet grown nor bird sung,
    He planned us to be his special creatures,
To become complete without any flaw,
    Overflowing with the gift of love.

Great and marvellous are your deeds,
    King of all ages!
Beautiful are the works of your fingers,
    Lord of the beginning and the end!

It was his secret purpose and joy
    Through the power of the lovely Christ,
To destine us to become his own children,
    Releasing love and praise in all places.
For our liberation and fulfilment is certain
    Through the shedding of the blood of the Beloved.

Wonderful is the name of Jesus Christ,
    Father of all mercy!
Beautiful is the voice that brings our freedom,
    God of liberty!

Through the life of Jesus, freely offered,
    All our sins have been forgiven;
We see the wealth of amazing grace
    Poured upon us without limit,
Bringing a knowledge greater than all learning,
    And insight deeper than all sages and prophets.

Who shall not marvel at your wisdom,
　　God of our salvation!
Who shall not tremble at the cost,
　　Father of the Crucified!

The Divine secret, so long obscured,
　Prepared from the beginning in Christ,
Has now been shown openly to us,
　Implemented when the time was ripe:

Everything, absolutely everything in the universe,
　In the expanses of eternity and the confines of time,
Is to be brought into a glorious harmony
　Through the Christ, our incomparable Lord!

Glorious is your secret,
　　Reconciling God!
Let prophets, apostles, and martyrs,
　　And everything in earth and heaven,
Exult with unbounded joy
　　From generation to generation, evermore!

Reflections, Wynyard Lake, Tasmania.

Who Am I?

I am the joyful shepherds
   who heard the angels sing —
And the preoccupied innkeeper
   whose stable housed a King.

I am the three wise men
   who travelled from afar —
And the terrible King Herod
   who feared your rising star.

I am the disciples who followed
   the new friend they had found —
And the fussy scribes who found you
   too uncomfortable to have around.

I am the prodigal son
   come home to my Father's place —
And the righteous elder brother
   who resented the gift of grace.

I am the rich man who lived it up,
   spurning the beggar at the gate —
And bustling, touchy Martha,
   who couldn't bear to sit and wait.

I am the crowd that gathered,
   wanting to put a crown on your head —
And I am the devil who tempted you
   with pleas for power, signs, and bread.

I am Zacchaeus who unprepared
   had you as guest and Saviour —
and the stiff-necked Pharisees
   who grumbled about your behaviour.

I am the crowd who cried 'Hosanna' —
    And Peter who let you down;
The police who did their duty well,
    and laughed at your thorny crown.

I am John who stood near your cross —
    And the soldiers who nailed the wood;
Mary who found an empty tomb —
    and Thomas, a risen Lord!

I am the apostles who took your Gospel
    to people everywhere.
Lord, I am just one hungry child
    with bread to eat and to share.

Jesus Is King

Come, join to praise with morning light:
    Our loving King!
Let grateful voices sound with might:
    Our loving King!
Let children's voices tell their praise,
While aged lips extol your ways,
Let every tongue in joy unite:
    Our loving King
    To you we bring
    Our praise!

Let songs like this ring through our land:
    Our loving King!
From coastal farms and inland sand:
    Our loving King!
Let all our nation thankful raise
Its voice in glad tumultuous praise:
    Our loving King
    To you we bring
    Our praise!

Let earth's great millions thund'rous shout:
    Our loving King!
Let this song spin the clouds about:
    Our loving King!
We'll always shout and sing your praise
While years flit by like passing days,
Until time runs its last hour out:
    Our loving King
    To you we bring
    Our praise!

PART II
The Shame and the Glory

Holiness

I saw the Lord
weeping
with Aboriginal mothers
around shanties
and reservations
where children learn little
except early death
or from their fathers
the way of despair
and toxic bitterness —
    weeping.

   Holy, holy, holy is the Lord of hosts;
   The whole earth is full of his glory.

I saw the Lord
gasping
for breath in those churches
wherever shallow worshippers
mouth blessing on the hungry
then drive home
to overfills of protein
and sport on the TV —
    gasping.

   Holy, holy, holy is the Lord of hosts;
   The whole earth is full of his glory.

I saw the Lord
hoping
in students scanning open books
roughly asking why
why
why
searching deep into friendly eyes
for seeds of truth
worth living for
and dying —
    hoping.

Holy, holy, holy is the Lord of hosts;
The whole earth is full of his glory.

I saw the Lord
agonizing
through corridors and chambers
of Canberra
where hollow men
salute expediency
consult the opinion polls
so that our future
will be the past repeated
spreading stench like the last —
    agonizing.

Holy, holy, holy is the Lord of hosts;
The whole earth is full of his glory.

I saw the Lord
angry
whenever church councils and committees
tardily
face agenda lifelessly
with no fire in the gut
no hope in the eye
no readiness to lose all
in the Kingdom which
comes first —
    angry.

Holy, holy, holy is the Lord of hosts;
The whole earth is full of his glory.

O Lamb of God, who takes away the sins of the world,
    Have mercy upon us.
O Lamb of God, who takes away the sins of the world,
    Have mercy upon us.
O Lamb of God, who takes away the sins of the world,
    Grant us your peace.

Penitence

We watch and wait, Lord,
   we scan the horizon for a sign of change —
Like farmers in a year of drought,
   looking for a change of heart in Australia.
For our countrymen have become like crows;
   like scavengers that live off the disasters of others;
Like hawks hovering,
   looking for smaller creatures to devour.

They care not for the exploited or unemployed,
   their only interest is in their own pay-packet.
Big business is as rapacious as a pack of dingoes;
   strong unions lie in wait like the crocodile.
Survival of the fattest is the national creed;
   little people are the ones who bleed.

Tanks and windmill, New South Wales.

We scorn the land rights of Aborigines,
   and admit a minimum of refugees.
People of low ability are labelled bludgers;
   loyal men in their fifties are declared redundant.
New Australians are given the dirtiest jobs;
   and their culture is mocked and despised.
Overseas aid is tied to political strings;
   we gamble a million times more than we give to the poor.

Lord, we wait and watch for change of heart,
   torn by anger and grief at ourselves and others.
We, the ugly Australians, pray for salvation,
   for the Rain that can make our centre bloom again.
We, the sick Australians, pray for healing,
   for the Prescription that can cure our festering sores.

How Long?

Psalm 13

How long will it be, Lord, before you remember me?
   How long will you remain incognito?
How long must I daily grieve and suffer inwardly?
   How long shall my opponents crow over me?

Look at me, Lord, and give me an answer;
   let me see some light, or I might as well be dead.
My opponents will consider me defeated,
   laughing when they watch me tremble.

Yet I will still trust your mercy,
   celebrating in my heart your salvation,
Singing to the true God
   who has been more than generous to me.

Rebellion

Some days we find it hard to love you, Lord;
    we smoulder with rebellion, even in church.
Your way of managing this world seems wrong;
    your love and justice appear to be missing.
From Ireland to Cambodia, Australia to Chile,
    we confront a tangle of suffering.
From New York to Peking, Canberra to Moscow,
    there is no clear path that leads to a better world.
The world shudders with injustice and torture;
    hatreds and fear spawn the agony of wars.
All the efforts of nobler people bear poor fruit;
    prophets, seers, and poets die unfulfilled.
Well-meaning politicians are reduced to cynicism;
    their ideals perish under the weight of 'respectable' corruption.
Scientific discoveries are prostituted by pride, greed, and war;
    even gifted physicians serve the rich rather than the sick.

It seems your fault, Lord!
    You made this world where tragedies occur!
Why did you create the possibility of greed?
    Or the neglect of your Aboriginal children?
The neuroses that afflict high-rise living?
    And the stupidity of poker machines and the road toll?
You permitted the opening for graft and corruption;
    you allow injustice and starvation to continue.
In us you have placed a hunger for a better world,
    but we lack the ability to build that world.
None of us are able to put into practice all we believe;
    you let us wander among our broken promises.
Lord, to whom can we turn?
    Where can we find adequate resources?

Lord, if it were not for Jesus of Nazareth,
    we would have given up long ago.
If his forgiveness and renewal were removed,
    we would slip away into dark despair.

But because you have given us one proper man
　　in whom salvation takes glorious shape,
There is hope for us all,
　　there is joy at the end of the travail.
O let our lives become filled with his grace!
　　Weld our souls to the steel of his soul!
Transform our rebellion into renewed discipleship;
　　replace our anger with a fresh discipline.
Help us to see your love at work in darkest places,
　　and to recognize your glory in tiny victories!
O lead us into the new creation begun in Jesus!
　　Raise up your new nation among all nations!

Homes

Psalm 127

Unless home-life is built by the Lord,
　　the carpenter's efforts are useless;
Unless a nation trusts in God,
　　armies are quite worthless.
To work heavy overtime,
　　or to run two jobs at once
in order to get rich quickly,
　　is an exercise in futility.
For the Lord supplies our deepest needs,
　　and his gifts are as free as sleep.

Children are a favour from the Lord,
　　a family the loveliest reward.
Better than weapons to a soldier
　　are children to godly parents;
They are indeed a happy couple
　　who are hugged daily by tiny arms.
They shall never feel defeated
　　when doubts and fears assail them.

The Still Centre

When we want healing at the core of being,
   we turn to you, God of Christ Jesus!
When we discover the still centre of the storm,
   it's you we find there, most wonderful Lord!

Sometimes our life seems a jumble of fragments;
   nothing matches nor fits together.
A feeling of being lost floods in like a tide;
   anxiety erodes our inmost selves.
We are permeated by seeping discomfort,
   as if we are at odds with our own soul.
All good humour hides itself away;
   peace and joy become mere memory.

Then it is we find it hard to care for others;
   we are too distracted to notice their needs.
Self-giving becomes an impossible calling;
   love shrinks into a four-letter word.
Even our capacity to listen closes down;
   our counsel is but jagged lumps of yesterday.

Ayers Rock, Northern Territory.

Father of Christ, we refind ourselves only in you;
    nowhere else do we find true integration.
At home with you we are at home with ourselves;
    in your love we begin to care for ourselves.
Your peace passes all understanding;
    your joy liberates the laughter within us.
We begin to hear, and care for others again;
    love is shared as from a depthless source.
How shall we thank you, most loving God?
    Can gratitude ever find adequate voice?
Still Centre of all the storms, we worship you!
    Crux of the universe, we glorify you!

The Only Hope

Psalm 5

Lord, you hear what I'm saying;
    you see what I'm thinking.
My only hope is for you to keep listening;
    you're the only One to whom I can turn.
Every morning my tongue feels for the best words;
    when I wake up I want to praise you.
You don't find pleasure in our mistakes;
    for nothing unloving can live with you.
Stupidity cannot stand up to you;
    those who hurt others shall taste your displeasure.
For my part, I will come to church celebrating your love;
    in gratitude I'll turn my face to the Table and the Cross.
Lead me, Lord, in genuine goodness;
    show me the way which goes straight ahead.
Come, everyone who loves God, celebrate with me;
    join me in a shout of joy!
You care for them too;
    may they find utter happiness in you.
For you give happiness to all loving people;
    your caring love is stronger than steel.

When We Are Feeling Down

Hey, everyone! Celebrate the Lord with me!
Join in, all you people who are feeling down!
Today is a time for affirming life,
each hour a commitment in hope.
When we are feeling low, that is the time for praise;
when our feelings mock us, our mind should give thanks.

On some days it is easy to worship,
for love and gratitude arrive eagerly,
Bringing heart-warming joy,
like children coming to a party.
Such praise is as native as the grevillea;
as natural as mallee blossom in springtime.

But there are other days when we see only the shadows:
the grime on buildings, the papers in gutters,
The cat stalking the blackbird,
the wind tearing a limb from the red gum,
The politician's absurd duplicity,
the unionist's stupidity and the businessman's greed.
Music on the radio is banal and absurd,
while newspapers headline the horrible;
Even the church seems to have cliques
where people love darkness rather than light.

Come, my friends, you know such times;
some days are soaked with gloom.
But shall we submit to life's shadows?
Shall we add to life's sorrows?
When darkness appears to reign,
that is the time to trust light.
When ugliness flaunts itself,
then is the moment for beauty.
If life snarls up in meaninglessness,
there is space for Christ's purposefulness.
When our path is stained with the suffering of man,
then shall we recognize Christ's presence.

My friends, have we made our moods into an idol?
  Shall we obey our feelings rather than God?
Hey, everyone! Make a stand with me!
  Defy your feelings and trust the Lord!
Call the bluff of cloudy chaos
  and make room for some life and shape;
In the midst of gloom, God speaks,
  Saying, 'Let there be light'.

Healing

Psalm 51

In your dependable love, Lord, I find healing;
  your unconditional acceptance removes my shame.
I want to be washed clean,
  to be made like new again.
Excuses for my sins are no good;
  my failure to love stands out a mile.
Worst of all, my lovelessness hurts you;
  what I fail to do for others adds to your pain.
When I think of you suffering,
  I quite justly feel most miserable.
But you don't hold it against me;
  you help me recover from my shame.
Lord, I want to be remade deep down;
  the current of life in me needs transforming.
Lord, my feelings need purifying;
  my attitudes and ideas must be reshaped.
Above all things, Lord, don't ever leave me;
  nor remove your saving Spirit from me.
Help me to delight in you more than anything else;
  in the liberty you give, may I stand up straight.

His Arms

Lord, your arms reached out
   to save a vagrant world:
   baby arms, embracing mother and father;
   boyish hands, holding a sacred scroll;
   brotherly arms, helping family and friends.

Lord, your arms reached out
   to signal a new beginning:
   acknowledging the Baptist at the Jordan,
   beckoning to fishermen by the sea,
   pointing to the narrow way that leads to life.

Lord, your arms reached out
   to stop the pain around you:
   straightening curved spine and crippled leg,
   opening the eyes of the blind,
   touching the skin of the lonely leper.

Lord, your arms reached out
   to welcome those who despised themselves:
   sharing bread with outcasts,
   writing in the dust for a broken woman,
   shaking the hand of Zacchaeus.

Lord, your arms reached out
   to express the divine anger:
   pushing Peter out of your way,
   shaking a fist at arrogant Pharisees,
   cleansing the temple with a whip.

Lord, your arms reached out
   to bear the burden of man's sin:
   washing the feet of fickle disciples,
   carrying a cross through jeering crowds,
   embracing the world with crucified arms.

Lord, your arms reached out
    to break the bonds of awful death:
    greeting the astounded disciples,
    showing Thomas the wounds of love,
    sending your witnesses to the ends of the earth.

Lord, your arms reach out
    transcending time and space:
    beckoning us to turn and follow,
    serving us the bread and wine,
    touching us with renewing grace.

Lord, your hands shall reach out
    gathering folk from every nation:
    breaking down walls that divide us,
    reconciling humanity through your cross,
    handing to the Father the finished new creation!

Our Work

Lord, our attitude to work changes with our moods;
    we are as variable as the weather.
Some days we enjoy every moment of our work;
    other days we feel tired and resentful of it.
There are mornings when we dread the thought of getting up;
    but there are also times when we go to work gladly.

Lord, some of us get paid for doing the things we enjoy;
    others must work at distasteful tasks for their living.
Some of us work with kind and interesting people;
    others must work with sour and ugly characters.
Some who long for company must work alone;
    others who yearn for privacy must work with a crowd.

Sheepshearing, New South Wales.

Lord, whether we work for love or pleasure,
 or whether it is only for duty or money,
We thank you for the privilege of daily work,
 for the rewards of labour in whatever form.
In a world where millions are unemployed,
 we count ourselves as richly blessed.

As products of the work of a loving Creator,
 we thank you for skills of eye, brain, and hand.
As friends of the carpenter's Son of Nazareth,
 we offer to you our work as an act of praise.
As children of the Spirit who has never ceased to work,
 we seek to honour you in everything we do.

Happy People

Psalm 128

Happy are those who honour God,
 sharing his ways.
You will work and eat;
 fun and goodness will be yours.
Wife and husband, like fruitful trees,
 shall tap the intimate joys of home.
Your children shall be like sturdy seedlings,
 growing straight and tall.
That's how it will happen
 for those who honour God!
Happiness will come from his Church,
 and your worship will be a delight.
All the days of your life
 you will delight in his growing family.
Peace be to God's people!
 Peace be to his Church!

The Body

1 Corinthians 12

We are the Body of Christ,
    each one of us a limb or organ.
Let us glorify God in the use of our bodies,
    which is a most reasonable worship.

All who are Christ's hands —
    gifted in healing or helping,
    making music or machinery,
    painting, polishing or planting:
  glorify God in your bodies.

All who are Christ's eyes —
    studying society and the Scriptures,
    noticing newcomer and nonentity,
    at microscopes, murals, and mathematics:
  glorify God in your bodies.

All who are Christ's ears —
    aware of weeping and wandering,
    hearing harmony and hypocrisy,
    listening to laughter, logic and the lonely:
  glorify God in your bodies.

You who are Christ's lips —
    teaching, training, testifying,
    singing, selling, satirizing,
    encouraging, enlightening, engendering:
  glorify God in your bodies.

You who are Christ's feet —
    walking, working, waiting,
    striding into service and sacrifice,
    running to receive a prodigal:
  glorify God in your bodies.

You who are Christ's heart —
    feeling the fellowship of faith,
    agonizing with Aboriginal and alcoholic,
    loving the least and the last:
 glorify God in your bodies.

If one suffers, we all suffer;
    if one flourishes, we all rejoice.
We are the Body of Christ;
    let us glorify God in this holy Body.

Brother

Poor restless son
    of a tired mother-land,
wanders the gutters,
and — shaken — stutters,
    craving a brother's hand.

Pleads this son
    of an apathetic mother;
    patronized by his brother
with a one-dollar conscience,
or the supercilious nonsense
    of a pair of old boots
    and moth-wise suits.

Alone this brother
    waits in the park;
papers restless in the dusk-wind's sighing
chorus an infinite anguished crying,
    which the coming dark
    can't smother.

God's Strength
Psalm 121

When I gaze at the ancient mountains,
   their huge strength steadies my trembling.
The strength of the Lord made the galaxies,
   and shaped this dear old planet.
You can never stumble out of his care;
   he who loves you never falls asleep.
The One who looks after you is awake,
   always alert to the cries of his children.
Your God cares for you,
   closer than your own right hand.
Even the fiery sun will not harm you,
   nor the barren face of the moon.
God will keep you going in hard times;
   he'll treasure your very being.
When you leave for work in the morning,
   and when you return home at evening,
He will surely be with you,
   this day and for ever.

The Nut, Stanley, Tasmania.

When

Lord, when my prayers are like a gibber plain,
and my soul like spinifex —
drench me with a downpour of mercy!

When I take things for granted
and gratitude goes to sleep —
put a new song on my tongue
till I praise as naturally as the bellbird.

When life's abrasive pressures fray me,
loosening my hold on the Still Centre —
tell me again about sparrows and magpies,
about wild lilies and pink heath,
and the Father who knows my needs.

When my miserly soul begrudges love,
complaining about importunate people,
or hides smugly in the folds of apathy —
put into my hands a crown of thorns,
and show me again what love can make
with two pieces of wood and a few nails.

Wave Rock, near Hyden, Western Australia.

This Mystery

There is a mystery
  wherein there is no confusion.
It is truth,
  which is never devised.
It is righteousness
  antecedent to every good deed.
It is justice, immeasurably larger
  than the righting of wrongs.
It is the beginning
  which is the end.
It is the weakness
  which is the only power.
It is the search
  which follows the finding.

The mystery is beneath the dignity
  of rulers, businessmen, and scientists,
Yet it is the origin
  of every beautiful deed
  which has ever enhanced the dignity of man.
It is the simplest idea,
  the most natural of deeds.

The fools of the world
  do not recognize this mystery
  even though they see its embodiment.
They do not follow the music,
  even though it surpasses all harmony.
They refuse to take it home
  because it cannot be bought.
They die without its joy
  because it's not the image of themselves.

The mystery dwells in you,
  and you in it.
Only when you love your own being
  can you know its truth.
And only when you trust its truth
  can you love your own being.

Here is the paradox
  which evades mere mind —
  but which envelops the whole being,
  inducting it into grace, mercy, and peace.

It confounds the philosophizers
  and scandalizes the religious.
It reveals itself
  in the deeds of a condemned rabbi,
  despised and rejected of men,
  a man of sorrows
  and acquainted with grief.

Judgment

Psalm 50

The only God has spoken;
   the Lord gives his word.
From beyond sunrise and sunset
   he calls the world to judgment;
From his city shines penetrating light,
   the radiance of sheer perfection.
Certainly he is coming,
   certainly he won't be silenced.
The fire of his presence will melt excuses;
   the wind of his spirit will break our defences.
Heaven and earth shall be summoned
   to the inescapable hour of reckoning.
Even his faithful friends must come,
   and the people of his covenant.
The skies shall ring with judgment
   when God delivers his verdict.

God's word is plain for the hypocrite;
   his grounds are completely clear:
'How dare you quote texts,
   you who evade renewal!
How can you glibly mouth my words,
   you who turn your backs?
You approve society's lawful thieves;
   you share in love's devaluation.
You are stuffed to the teeth with evil;
   your tongue frames smooth lies.
Every day you hound your brothers
   and stab your sisters in the back.
This and far worse you have done.
   Should I now keep quiet?
You even try to mould me in your own image!
   Openly shall I discipline you!'

Think about it,
   you who forget your God.
If the Lord tears your defences to pieces,
   who is there to save you?

But those who gladly give him all
    shall know a glorious freedom!
Those who worship in word and deed
    will see the salvation of God!

Dependable Word

Psalm 12

Help, Lord. What can we trust?
    Where is a dependable word?
Words no longer give communication,
    but are tuned for exploitation.
Men look us in the eye and lie;
    with secret motives they flatter us.
Lord, shut the lips of confidence men,
    and the tongues that exploit our pride.
Silence all media that twist the truth,
    the ad-men who can sell us destruction.

Listen! The Lord speaks,
    the only reliable voice is heard:
'Because of the plunder of the poor,
    and the groans of the lost,
I am among you, my people;
    I will protect you from the arrogant'.

This is the word we can trust,
    the pure word of Immanuel.
Like sterling silver is his word,
    refined seven times over.
He alone keeps his word,
    and saves us from the words around us.
Though scheming men oppose us,
    though voices cajole or bully us,
His word is the only word of life,
    the Word that endures for ever.

God Hidden and Present

Isaiah 63, 64

Lord, look from the place of your holiness,
    see us from the heights of your glory!
Where is your inspiration and courage?
    Your inflaming, caring love?
The saints and prophets cannot see us,
    Augustine and Luther cannot help us.
But you, Lord, are our Father,
    our kinsman from of old.
Why do you allow us to lose our way?
    Why let us become hard and godless?
For your servants' sake, do something!
    We are your own family!
Why permit despisers to stamp on our church?
    Why let them trample over sacred things?
We are treated as though outside your rule,
    like those who never received your call.

Why not leave your hiding and come among us,
    till the mountains quake in your presence!
Come, blazing like a forest fire,
    and bubbling like boiling water.
That would make unbelievers know you;
    the nations would tremble at your presence.
You have done unexpected things before,
    when the mountains shook at your coming.

We have indeed rebelled, and you have disciplined us,
    yet we continue on evil ways.
We have all become corrupted;
    even our goodness is as dirty rags.
We wither like old leaves;
    like the wind our sins sweep us away.
Nobody calls your name with total love,
    or clings to you in complete trust.
So you hide your presence from us,
    and allow our sins to consume us.

Today, Lord, we are as clay;
    you are the Master Potter.
We are your handiwork;
    you are our dear Father.

Ear has never heard,
    nor eye ever seen,
Any other god coming to the aid
    of those who patiently wait for him!
You welcome those who rejoice in goodness,
    and meet with those who remember your ways!

Hunger and Thirst

Unfathomable God,
you have given us hunger —
and the food to satisfy us,
the experience of thirst —
and the drink to quench it.
Can it be that,
hungering and thirsting for you,
we shall be denied satisfaction?

Water of life and Bread of heaven,
give us stubbornness in our seeking,
persistence in our partaking,
honesty in our questioning,
so that we may not despair
nor abandon the effort to pray;
not chase attractive substitutes,
nor fail to listen
to your witnesses.

Help us to creatively meditate
on the wisdom of Scripture —
the ugliness of human sin
and the sadness of death,
the wonder of divine love
and the life of Christ —
until our inner lives expand
and we begin to understand.

O loving God,
the beyond who is among us,
the thirst and the quenching,
the hunger and the satisfaction,
help us to live out our own prayers,
trusting you more lovingly,
listening more carefully,
and obeying more faithfully.

Then will our thirsty desert
blossom like a rose;
in our wilderness
we will eat manna;
in our seeking
we shall be surely found.
The glory of the Lord shall possess us,
the splendour of our God be revealed,
and we shall truly rest.

Sunrise, Moralana Scenic Drive, South Australia.

Forsaken?

My God! My God, why have you forsaken us —
forsaken us in the cry of the crucified!
In his horrible helplessness
we are doubly helpless,
suffering by the million
and dying
alone.

My God! The nails that pierced Jesus cruelly,
surely pierce our one humanity;
the taunts from bystanders are ours:
the secret doubt that all
ends in an empty whimper,
bereft of light and
love.

My God! That his life should thus mercilessly end,
surrounded by such malignant rejection,
loved only by a frightened few
watching in fear,
leaves us all in
dereliction and
despair.

My God! Into that cold stone tomb
fall all our noblest human dreams;
the idealism of youth sinks
low in the deep shadows,
and even desperate defiance
in the darkness
weeps.

Dear God! On that black Friday you did not forsake us!
Not Jesus, nor any other desolate child of man!
That day you entered all our forsakenness,
tasting bitter dereliction and death,
shaping the valley of the shadow
to become an avenue of
hope.

We praise you, O God! We acknowledge you to be the Lord!
Despised and rejected, man of sorrows and grief,
great and marvellous are your deeds!
Wounded for our transgressions,
bruised for our iniquities,
God is with us!
Hallelujah!

Sweet and Sour

In this mysterious union of energy
   which we call humanity,
The black and the gold
   are so closely woven
That one cannot remove the pain
   without undoing the joy.

The gentle Buddhist,
   discovering this truth,
Removes both black and gold
   from his daily experience,
And calls the unsweetened, unbittered vestige
   the only peace.

Not so our Jesus,
   who embraces both
   with strong bleeding arms,
Affirming both Creator and creation
   as lovable —
And salvation as intrinsic
   to both the broken body and the shed blood,
   and the joy of wedding celebrations.

In this sweet and sour
   we spend our days.
In the unfolding of his purposes
We find our Lord giving the breath of life,
   while always
   his tears soak us,
   his joy uplifts us,
   and his love fills us.

PART III
These Are the Days

Advent 1

Come, Lord Jesus

'Come, Lord Jesus.'
'Come!' say the Spirit and the Church.
'Come!' let each hearer reply.
This same Jesus,
whom we love but no longer see,
shall come again in glory
to judge the living and the dead.
    Come, Lord Jesus.

Unexpected as a thief,
unexpected as a midnight guest,
unexpected as the lightning:
    Even so come, Lord Jesus.

To expose the hidden guilt,
to expose the schemes of men,
to expose the powers of darkness:
    Even so come, Lord Jesus.

Bringing judgment to the arrogant,
bringing discipline to the unfaithful,
bringing rebuke to the apathetic:
    Even so come, Lord Jesus.

Giving rest to the weary,
giving healing to the sick,
giving forgiveness to the repentant:
    Even so come, Lord Jesus.

Like light in darkness,
like water for the thirsty,
like a bridegroom for a bride:
    Even so come, Lord Jesus.

As the stiller of storms,
as the giver of living bread,
as the friend of sinners:
    Even so come, Lord Jesus.

With a kingdom for the poor,
with a world for the meek,
with rejoicing for the persecuted:
    Even so come, Lord Jesus.

Fulfilling the prayers of martyrs,
fulfilling the work of the cross,
fulfilling the resurrection joy:
    Even so come, Lord Jesus.

Mallacoota Beach, Victoria.

Advent 2

The Word within the Word

Most wonderful God, this is your world,
the fruit of your creating and redeeming word;
the word which shaped the history
out of which the Bible was written.

> For the Word from the beginning
> speaking as One who has authority,
> word of life:
> we thank you, Lord most high!

You spoke through many writers —
some simple and some sophisticated,
poets, historians, shepherds, and princes —
each inspired to pass the word on.

> For the Word which is a lamp,
> guide to our feet, beacon on our path,
> word of light:
> we thank you, Lord most high!

The scribes of many generations who toiled,
patiently reproducing the sacred scrolls,
you nurtured, God of the ages.
Through them your treasure came down to us.

> For those who delighted in your Word
> and forgot not your laws,
> word of truth:
> we thank you, Lord most high.

Translators you gave us, servants of the Word,
conveying the Good News in our native tongue;
Bede, Wycliffe, and the sages of King James,
Moffatt, Phillips, and scholars of today.

> For the Word that cannot be bound,
> skilfully spoken in due season,
> word like fire:
> we thank you, Lord most high.

You have given our nation your Word;
in Australia the Scriptures abound.
You have provided bookshops and Bible Societies,
and given us the freedom to share it.

For the Word that dwells richly in us,
and that never returns empty,
word that brings faith:
we thank you, Lord most high.

Wonderful God, we rejoice in the Gospel,
the witness of the Bible to Jesus Christ,
the Word within the words,
speaking a saving word to all people.

For the Word made flesh,
glorious Word who dwells among us,
word of love:
we praise you, Lord most high.

Advent 3

Prepare the Way of the Lord

There is a voice that cries in the wilderness,
the prophet word demanding change:
'Prepare the way of the Lord;
fill in the gullies, level the ridges,
straighten the crooked, move the mountains.
God's glory shall be revealed
and every eye shall see it.'

   Smooth the rough places,
   move the mountains;
   let God's glory be displayed!

In the wilderness of our cities,
furrowed by freeways and shaded by skyscrapers,
where hollow people jostle without love
or get lost in the wastes of suburbia,
where anonymous persons hide in flats,
or broken men queue up at hostels
for a bed and respite from dereliction:
Prepare the way of the Lord.

   Smooth the rough places,
   move the mountains;
   let God's glory be displayed!

In the wilderness of our countryside,
where little farmers eke out existence
while the rich accumulate massive farms
and city people play games on farmlets,
where once-proud towns shrink into shabbiness,
their sons and daughters drained off to the cities,
and unemployed blacks drink behind pubs:
Prepare the way of the Lord.

   Smooth the rough places,
   move the mountains;
   let God's glory be displayed!

In the wilderness of our schools and colleges,
the training-ground for survival of the fittest,
where the young learn almost everything
except how to become children of God,
expanding in mind but not in soul;
where young people earn diplomas, but little wisdom,
or graduate with honours in all but love:
Prepare the way of the Lord.

    Smooth the rough places,
    move the mountains;
    let God's glory be displayed!

In the wilderness of our politics,
a field of stones and shabby fame,
where some blatantly offer election bribes
or have the gall to say they're the greatest,
where caring members can get mauled by power-brokers
and are relegated to the back benches
till cynicism breeds like a horrible virus:
Prepare the way of the Lord.

    Smooth the rough places,
    move the mountains;
    let God's glory be displayed!

In the wilderness of our religions
where theological fashions come and go,
buildings and crowds persist as status-symbols,
and pomp and circumstance are high on the ratings,
where evangelism can be considered poor taste,
prayer and sacrifice as optional extras,
and even Jesus is feared as 'extremist':
Prepare the way of the Lord.

    Smooth the rough places,
    move the mountains;
    let God's glory be displayed!

Voice in the wilderness, what shall we do?
Prophet of the Lord, what is the word?
'Turn, turn, turn to the Lord;
you who have two suits, give to the naked;
if you eat well, share with the hungry;
in business and authority, deal with compassion —
and be ready for the One who comes with fire.'

Smooth the rough places,
move the mountains;
let God's glory be displayed!

Nullarbor Highway, South Australia

Advent 4

He Comes

Psalm 24

He comes to his own world,
  though his own will not receive him.
Everything already belongs to him
  and the people of every nation.
From sea to sea he created it;
  all living things are his joy.

Can any of us dare face him?
  Or keep our poise in his presence?
If our hands had never harmed another,
  if our motives were perfectly pure,
If we had never been seduced by vanity,
  if no trace of deceit lingered in us,
Then we would boldly receive him,
  confidently seeking his blessing.

Corrupt we all are, yet we seek him;
  our generation searches for a god.
We are creatures who are always restless,
  seeking elusive security and peace.
We look for his face in our heroes;
  vainly we search in our libraries.

Lift up your tired heads!
  Open up your weary eyes!
The King of glory comes among us;
  he enters the gates of our humanity.
Who is this King of glory?
  The Lord who stoops to conquer,
The Lord of Shepherds and poor men,
  he is the King of glory!

Lift up your tired heads!
  Open your weary eyes!
The King of glory comes to you.
  Who is this King of glory?
The Lord of countless hosts,
  he is our King of glory!

The Leap Forward

Lord, shall Christmas come again
distracting us momentarily
from the boasts and myths
of that Babel we call civilization,
giving us a few days playing
at worshipping the Mystery —
before we rush back
to the world of contemporary fantasy
where diseased minds pretend
the real action is?

Lord, the things we laud as progress,
and name as giant steps forward,
are only the fancy footwork
of those who dance on the same spot,
dazzling the eyes that look on
with smart improvisations —
until we fail to see
how little we step forward
and how rarely we leap.

Lord, yours is the only advance.
That potent Bethlehem gift
is a tiny, weak thing
unable to walk, stand, or even sit —
yet in the hour of birth
leaping forward over ages,
and inviting us to follow
in this new and holy way
where even our few steps forward
release joy among herald angels.

Lord, now dawns our day of progress!
*Little son of God, laid in a manger,
we adore your coming!
Now God is our image, of our flesh and blood!
You are our Saviour and brother
who lies in a cot.
You lie in our misery,
share all our needs,
and assure us of glory!
Hallelujah!

* Thoughts from Martin Luther.

On Christmas Eve

Glory to God in the highest,
   and on earth peace, goodwill toward men!

The dry grass has turned light brown,
   crackling under footsteps like crisp paper.
Soak-hoses and sprinklers are at work,
   greening gardens and preserving shrubs.
The starlings arrive for a drink,
   while two brown doves take a shower.
In the old palm trees the sparrows gossip,
   and from the gum trees cicadas sing.

The highways are already thick with cars,
   packed with parents, presents, children, and pets.
In city parks crowds gather at dusk
   to sing by candlelight the much-loved carols.
Near midnight many stream into churches,
   ordinary people sharing an extraordinary faith:
Glorifying again the Word made flesh,
   tasting the royal Bread and priceless Wine.

Tomorrow the summer sun will wake us early,
   the few hours' sleep swiftly fled.
Even then, children will be out on the footpaths,
   their scooters, prams, and bikes sparkling.
At church, family worship will have many guests —
   cousins, grandparents, new toy bears, and dolls!
Outside church, more cards, kisses, and greetings —
   'Merry Christmas' under the hot morning sun.

By midday the aroma of turkey and mint peas
   will blend with the fragrance of fruit salad and puddings;
The scent of pollens on a warm summer wind,
   mixed with the smell of pine needles and fruit punch.
Chatter, eating, and laughter — all blending
   with fond memories of other years:
The personal, spiritual, and secular
   poured together into one incarnational celebration.

It's Christmas Eve again in this lucky country;
  Christ's birthday awaited under evening skies.
Dear God, what a holy day tomorrow will be!
  What a celebration of life and love!

With the whole church on earth and in heaven,
  we join in the angels' song:
'Glory to God in the highest,
  and on earth peace, goodwill toward men'.

Christmas

Rejoice, Australia, in God your Saviour!
    Celebrate today the Christmas Gift.
From Launceston, Broome, Cairns, and Mt Gambier,
    let the story be told and the carols uplift.
In the hot dusty inland, sing his glad music;
    on crowded beaches, remember his birth.
Christ Jesus has come among us for ever;
    his birthday offers a new hope on earth.

Let mountain ash, karri, and blackwood salute him.
    jacaranda, banksia, fern, and flame tree.
Let dry places blossom with blue cattle bushes,
    and plains turn red with Sturt desert pea.
Rejoice, you mountains, bushland, and forest;
    heath and waratah make gay jubilee!

Run like the wind, long-legged emu,
    to all remote creatures carry the word!
Leap for joy, wallaby, kangaroo, and quokka;
    dance, elegant brolga and shy lyre bird!
Chatter the story, bright lorikeets and parrots,
    give all flying things the news you have heard!

Join the celebration, all human population —
    late arrivals to the great south land!
All families, come and worship in country and city,
    at inland homesteads, or on warm beach sand!
Black people, make him your best corroborees!
    Descendants of pioneers, sing your praise!
New Australians from Asia, Africa, and Europe,
    offer the heritage of your ancient ways!

Rejoice, Australia, in God your Saviour;
    exult, old continent and young nation!
In the arms of the Virgin, see your salvation,
    the destiny awaited for countless years.
Arise, and laugh, and dance, and sing,
    for the Antipodes, too, have a glorious King!

Your Day

Jesus, how strong
and irrepressible
is this your day.

Though hedged by greed
and masked by tinsel,
it has its say.

Our crowds disperse
and turn tired eyes
to where you lay.

Some spurn the sign.
Rapt, others find God
in human clay!

For the New Year

Sing to the Lord a New Year's song!
Give him the highest New Year honours:
Thank the Lord for the old year ended,
Trust him at the dawning of the new.
Lift our faces to the midnight sky and rejoice!
Let the Southern Cross be our pilgrim sign.

Praise the Lord for the things that endure;
Old things transcending the changing years:
The solid soil of our ancient land under our feet;
Incessant seas that wash our shores from Hobart to Darwin;
The morning sun rising on a familiar landscape;
The westerlies spinning windmills or dispersing city smog;
After rains, the dry Centre blossoming in profusion;
Trees on the Great Divide reaching tall for the sky;
Your divine purpose brooding over Australia,
Loving our land long before we shared it;
Your divine mercy encircling every person,
Speaking our names in a hundred different accents.
Among us the saving deeds of Jesus Christ —
The same yesterday, today, and for ever!

Praise the Lord for new possibilities being born,
New lights that gleam on every horizon:
The strengthening of faith and enlarging of vision;
The fellowship of Christ in success or failure;
Readiness to care for needy fellow-citizens —
The physically, socially, or spiritually handicapped;
Liberation from political and religious prejudice,
And a hearty commitment to the ways of Jesus;
The willingness to listen to the words of an opponent;
The courage to speak up when cowards become dumb;
The chance to break idols of possessions and position;
Worshipping the power that is made perfect in weakness;
Discarding personal day-dreams for the dreams of our Lord —
The same yesterday, today, and for ever!

Sing to the Lord a New Year's song!
Give him the choicest of New Year honours:
    As we greet one another with 'Happy New Year',
    Greet him as the Lord of every minute.
    For his call will be renewed each morning,
    And his peace shall be ours at close of every day.

Epiphany

Arise, Australia, arise,
　for your light has surely come!
The glory of the Lord is risen upon you,
　and the darkness cannot quench it.
We, too, have seen the rising of his star,
　and have come to worship him.
Jesus, light of the world, we honour you!
　Jesus, light in our national darkness, we need you!

Come, Prime Minister and Premier, stand in his light;
　parliaments and councils, learn his ways.
Come, business and trade unions, stand in his light;
　managers and shop stewards, hear his good news.

Let Sydney and Melbourne respond to his rising,
　Canberra and Darwin his freedom receive.
Let Perth and Hobart respond to his rising,
　Adelaide and Brisbane discover his love.

Turn, magistrate and judge, face his glory;
　lawyers and jurors, discover his laws.
Turn, teacher and professor, face his glory;
　graduates and students, give him your lives.

Let Port Hedland and Port Arthur respond to his rising,
　Gundagai and Coober Pedy receive his rare joy.
Let Broken Hill and Mt Isa respond to his rising,
　Goondiwindi and Dimboola share his new day!

Journey, farmer and grazier, to follow his star;
　shearers and stockmen, venture a prayer.
Journey, miner and timberman, to follow his star;
　powder-monkey and truckies, acquire his power.

Arise, Australia, arise and sing,
   your light has surely come!
The light and glory of a holy God
   in the face of Bethlehem's Son.
We, too, have seen the rising of his star,
   and have come to worship him.
O that men would praise the Lord for his goodness,
   and his wonderful works to the children of men!

Senator Neville Bonner.

Lent 1

The Way of the Cross

If anyone wants to come with me, he must forget self,
take up his cross every day, and follow me. Luke 9:23 (TEV)

Lord, this is a troublesome saying,
   heavy and hard.
We jealously protect our gains,
   always on guard.
The more we have the more we crave,
   success self-made.
When you speak of losing all,
   we are afraid.

Lord, this is an embarrassing saying
   for folk like us.
Even over the smallest disciplines
   we make a great fuss.
We are not made of the stuff of heroes,
   without complaints.
We are just your little people,
   not noble saints.

Lord, this is a persistent saying,
   giving no rest.
In mind and soul we know it is sane,
   offering the best.
By gaining and grasping we know we lose
   life's deeper scope.
The strange logic of your cross remains
   life's only hope.

Lord, this is a saving saying,
   divine outlay.
The path of the cross the only glory
   all the way.
Willing, though fearful, help us to bear it,
   not growing slack.
Laughing and crying, help us to follow,
   not turning back.

Following in His Ways

Psalm 25

Our Lord, on you I rest my very being;
  on you I stake my life.
Don't let me ever be ashamed,
  or discouraged by the success of opponents.
No person who follows you is disgraced —
  only those who are unfaithful.

Show me, Lord, the disciple's path;
  teach me your ways.
Saviour, lead me and coach me;
  every day I'll trust your saving love.
Remember your unfailing compassion,
  shown throughout the ages.

Recall not the faults of my youth;
  remember me in your saving grace.
You alone are good and true;
  therefore show wanderers the way to go.
You guide ordinary folk aright;
  you teach the timid your way.

Lord, your loving ways are sure
  to those who follow and obey.
Your purpose is shown to true worshippers,
  and we experience your covenant.
I keep my eyes on you always;
  only you can save my feet from trouble.

When I feel lonely or depressed,
  Lord, turn back and encourage me.
If I grieve within my heart,
  free me from my distress.
When you see my anxiety and doubt,
  forgive my every sin.

Lent 2

Not by Bread Alone

*Man cannot live on bread alone, but needs every
word that God speaks.* Matthew 4:4 (TEV)

I do have faith, but not enough. Help me to have more.
Mark 9:24 (TEV)

In a world where people live for pride,
eating the bread of vanity:
from the conceit that looks for public
    praise and honours;
from the vainglory that flaunts diplomas
    and degrees;
from the arrogance of religious and
    moral swagger;
from the insolence of supposed racial
    superiority,
save your children, Lord.

In a world where people live by force,
eating the bread of power:
from all attempts to manipulate
    our friends;
from the temptation to scorn a
    defeated opponent;
from the desire to use chance advantages
    to disadvantage others;
from leaders who love to rule
    more than to serve,
save your children, Lord.

In a world where people live by greed,
eating the bread of cupidity:
from envy of those
    with larger homes;
from selling our ethics
    for a few more dollars;

from trusting the stock-market
  more than the Scriptures;
from supporting only those charities
  which offer an income tax deduction,
save your children, Lord.

In a world where people live by pleasure,
eating the bread of sensuality:
from turning food
  into an extravagant habit;
from cluttering our homes
  with technological toys;
from using our sexuality
  for indulgent lust;
from loving things
  and using people,
save your children, Lord.

Sydney Domain

For the Affluent

Psalm 49

Hear this, all Australians!
　　Listen, all people on earth,
The teeming millions and every single person,
　　the affluent and the needy!
For I have a sane word to speak,
　　the truth from a full heart.

There are many who trust money,
　　and show off their wealth.
Yet none can ransom themselves,
　　nor bribe God for redemption.
To ransom their soul is far too costly,
　　for ever beyond their means.

Remember: even smart people die;
　　so, too, do the foolish and the callous.
All wealth is left for others;
　　our home becomes the grave —
the place where we must remain
　　though our name might linger on a business.

The privileged have no exemption;
　　like animals we all perish.
Such is the destiny of fools,
　　and of all who admire them.
Like sheep they flock to doom,
　　with death their only shepherd.

Do not stand in awe of a rich man,
　　who lives in an extravagant home.
He can take nothing with him when he dies;
　　his vainglory shall not follow him.
But God shall ransom his humble people;
　　he shall save us from the power of death.

Lent 3

Don't Tempt God

Psalm 82

God takes a stand in the council of heaven,
  to judge those who live like gods.

How long will you encourage injustice,
  and give benefits to evil men?
You should lift up the weak and the orphan,
  give rights to all downtrodden people.
You should rescue the weak and the poor,
  freeing them from the grip of exploiters.
But you do not want to know,
  you are not willing to understand;
You stroll in the darkness
  while the foundation of the world shakes!

I tell you, though you could be godlike,
  children of the Most High,
You shall soon die like all men,
  you shall fall like all proud men.

O God, take your stand and judge us!
  The nations are at your disposal!

Don't Test God

The scripture also says, 'Do not put the Lord your God to the test'. Matthew 4:7 (TEV)

You must not test the Lord your God,
   nor ask for a sign of his presence;
His commandments are already given,
   guide-posts on the road to life.
His sign is imbedded in our history,
   the child of a young woman — Immanuel.
Only a wicked and perverse generation
   dare seek a greater sign than this.

Christ-given signs of his presence are with us:
   the haunted eyes of the starving
   looking at the camera of the tourist,
   and the pitiful band of refugees
   through whom Christ cries to us.
   As we sit at plenteous tables,
   or sleep in secure comfort,
   should we ask for other signs?
   Dare we test the Lord our God?

His signs are in our hospitals:
   thousands of road-accident victims,
   some dying, but not quickly enough,
   and many with no future
   except wheelchairs, callipers, or mindless years.
   Dare we test the Lord our God
   by saying prayers
   and then driving carelessly
   on our streets and highways?

The signs are in our churches:
   ordinary people with simple faith
   who humbly extend themselves
   with an extraordinary compassion
   in a thousand little actions;
   the unpretentious, grass-roots love
   which asks for no reward.
   Dare we test the Lord our God
   by demanding signs more grand?

Precious signs are in the Supper:
   fruits of our toil and the generosity of God;
   where the grace of soil, rain, and sunshine
   condense in a chalice
   and a piece of daily bread;
   where people meet with an everloving Host.
   Dare we test the Lord our God
   by asking for signs more profound?

Lent 4

One Lord

Psalm 33

If you are joyful, show it to the Lord!
    Stand tall and praise him!
Let music tell your gratitude:
    organ and guitar, trumpet and drums.
Haven't you a new song to sing?
    Put your whole strength into it.

What the Lord tells you is true;
    whatever he does is dependable.
He has a passion for integrity and justice,
    and sufficient love to fill the world.
Happy our nation when the Lord is God,
    when our people respond to his call.

The universe was framed from his words;
    the galaxies are his thoughts.
All the oceans are his waterbag,
    the Indian and Tasman his finger-bowl.
Let everything tremble before the Lord,
    every person stand in awe!

He scatters the diplomacy of empires;
    the Lord foils the schemes of the cunning.
Nations are not saved by vast armies,
    nor soldiers by brute strength.
Tanks and rockets don't give safety;
    no one wins by military power.

The purposes of the Lord are infinite;
    his plans extend from age to age.
Intimately he shapes the life of all,
    and broods over every single soul.
He is well aware of those who honour him;
    those who put all hope in his free grace.

Come, everyone! Let us place our hope in him!
　　Let us love our helper and guardian.
Every fibre of our being rejoices in him,
　　trusting his healing name.
Lord, let your sure love reside with us,
　　for we have no hope or joy but you.

Crater Lake, Tasmania.

Lent 4

God Alone

*The scripture says, 'Worship the Lord your God
and serve only him!'* Matthew 4:10 (TEV)

Jesus, on your high mountain I paused;
    I paused, watched, and pondered.
Below were my countrymen
    scurrying from coast to coast
in a frenzy of activity,
    pouring out vast energy
in a fervent search for joy.

I saw them like hungry scavengers,
    tearing hills apart for iron or lead,
burrowing into mountains for copper and zinc,
    ransacking the countryside for bauxite and rutile;
and towns grew up and facilities flourished,
    bridges spanned chasms, and airports were levelled —
but rare were the signs of joy.

I saw them feverishly building their cities,
    shops, banks, supermarkets, and factories,
universities, schools, town halls, and skyscrapers,
    freeways, suburbs, ferries, and railways.
The traffic lights blinked and the hordes rushed,
    the motor cars reared and the neon signs flashed —
but rare were the sounds of joy.

I saw them at play in city and country,
    races at Flemington and 'pokies' at Paddington,
chasing leather footballs in three varieties,
    striding down fairways or riding the waves,
white-clad contestants at cricket, bowls, or tennis,
    and for every sportsman a thousand watching 'telly' —
yet rare were the songs of joy.

I saw them at politics, zealous and vehement,
    canvassing for votes and playing with power,
paying homage to position, policy, and 'party',
    dancing to the tune of the opinion polls.
Endless rumbling words, tactics and meetings,
    boasting and evading with no sign of shame —
but rare were the sessions of joy.

Lord, from your high mountain I saw my countrymen,
    my people whom I love and loathe,
whom I deeply trust but fear;
    their energy was surprising, their persistence impressive,
their homage to their gods was most sincere.
    Some wore emblems and some wore crosses —
but rare were the scenes of joy.

Lent 5

The Lost

*The Son of Man came to seek and to save
the lost.* Luke 19:10 (TEV)

Lord, we get lost so easily:
   in the course of conversation,
   at the house of a neighbour,
   with good advice on our lips,
we get lost in our wisdom
and lose the gift of truth.

Lord, we get lost so unexpectedly:
   in the hour of success,
   at the home of a friend,
   with hymns on our tongues,
we get lost in our importance
and lose the gift of joy.

Lord, we get lost so crudely:
   in the middle of our prayers,
   at the party or the club,
   with humour in our words,
we get lost in our adaptability
and lose the gift of peace.

Lord, we get lost so profoundly:
   in the cause of Christian duty,
   at the social justice meeting,
   or with consecrated bread in our hands,
we get lost in our righteousness
and lose the gift of love.

Lord, we are found so simply:
   in the moment of awareness,
   at the hour of taking stock,
   with hunger in our being,
we lose ourselves in grace
and find the gift of life.

From the Depths

Psalm 130

Out of deep anguish I cry to you, Lord;
    Lord, can you hear me?
To the groaning of my prayers
    please carefully listen.
If you, Lord, keep a record of sins,
    then none of us dare face you.
But in you we find forgiveness,
    therefore we can adore you.
I wait, with all my soul I wait,
    and hope for the word I need.
With all my soul I long for my Lord,
    more than night-watchmen waiting for dawn.
Like the weary looking for sunrise,
    let all God's people wait in hope.
For with the Lord there is pure love,
    with him is abundant liberty.
He alone can set us free
    from all our sins.

Lent 6

Hosanna

Zechariah 7 - 9

Sing and rejoice, daughters of God!
    Shout for joy, sons of the Father!
Here comes your King
    travelling to his victory;
Riding humbly on a donkey,
    on a foal not ridden before.
Hosanna! All joy to our King!
    To the one who comes in the name of the Lord!

But my countrymen will not cheer;
    my people grumble at his coming.
Though their idols are useless,
    and their heroes are deceivers,
Though they wander like lost sheep
    without a loving shepherd,
Yet they will not listen,
    nor obey the word of the Lord.

He speaks up for true justice:
    'Give loyalty and compassion;
Care for the orphan and the pensioner;
    aid the refugee and those in poverty;
Do not ruthlessly exploit,
    or plot trouble for each other'.
But people will not listen;
    they shrug their shoulders and prepare a cross.

Ride on in majesty, King of love;
    show us the way that leads to peace.
The Lord shall banish our armies;
    our armaments shall be destroyed.
He shall speak reconciliation to every nation,
    extending his love from sea to sea.
This Kingdom which seems impossible
    shall surely come to be.

Hosanna! Keep steady your hands!
   Hear the word of the Lord of hosts:
Love shall reign in the city of God,
   old people shall sit in its squares;
Its streets shall be filled with children
   playing without any fears.
The Lord will dwell with his people,
   and banish all sorrow and cares.

Palm Sunday service of worship and witness, Mt Waverley, Victoria, 1973.

Good Friday

Lord, truly you have borne our griefs
    and carried our sorrows.
On this most terrible and wonderful day,
    when the sun was dimmed
    and the earth shuddered in horror,
We know it.

Lord, no longer is it only the blood of our brother
    that cries out from the ground.
Today we hear the voice of the blood of God
    pleading from the soil
    with a claim which will never be silenced
Or ever defeated.

Lord, everywhere we go your holy blood speaks:
    from the rocky soil of Israel,
The green fields of Devon and the vineyards of the Rhine,
    out of the clays of Uganda,
    from the prairies of Canada and rice paddies of Vietnam:
The cry of love.

Lord, our homeland, too, shudders in loving recognition,
    everywhere is now Golgotha:
Yanchep and Wilpena, Gove, Burnie, and Kingaroy,
    sheep stations and dairy farms,
    Blue Mountains and Wimmera wheatlands, all cry with the blood
Of the crucified God.

Lord, if in love we offered you our homeland,
    it would be poor thanks;
If the whole wealth of Mother Earth were given,
    even that would be inadequate praise.
O you who bear our griefs and carry our sorrows,
We are yours!

Easter

Christ is risen!
   Christ is risen indeed!
Come, you States and territories, glorify the Lord!
   From coast to coast, tell of his love!
Today all our defeats are defeated,
   and death is swallowed up in victory!

Praise him, all you Aboriginal people,
   your humiliation is not for ever!
Praise him, all unwanted and unemployed people,
   your dejection shall be turned into joy!
Praise him, all prisoners in cells or in drug addiction,
   your liberation begins at the empty tomb!
Praise him, all despairing and cynical people,
   your fears are rolled away with the stone!
Praise him, all lonely and homesick migrants,
   your risen Lord walks Australian streets, too!
Praise him, all who hurt from fresh bereavements,
   your grief can be mingled with peace.
Praise him, all half-hearted Christians,
   your Lord makes all things new!

Christ is risen!
   He is risen indeed!
With angels and archangels, and all the company of heaven,
   let Australians glorify his holy name!
Today all our defeats are defeated,
   and death is swallowed up in victory!

Pentecost

Lord, you come
like the wind
and the earth grows
hale at your breath.
You brood
over the face of the waters,
and in the Body of the Church,
shaping
the world that is to be.

You arrive —
like the wind filling a thousand sails
on Sydney Harbour —
and fill
our slack churches
with new power
and vision.

Like moist air
carrying refreshing rain
to the Flinders Ranges,
clothing the valleys with red hops,
carpeting the slopes with purple and gold,
so your Spirit
brings the colour of Christ
into drab communities.

You sweep in,
fresh as sea breezes across Port Phillip
bringing relief and restoration
to a hot and tired city,
dispersing the smog,
encouraging us to breathe deeply again
of the Breath of life.

Sometimes you roar
like a hurricane,
tearing away
the flimsy structures
of our gaudy materialism,
demolishing us
to the Ground of our Being.

As strong as a summer wind
transporting a myriad of seeds
to impregnate distant plains
with new patterns of life,
so you seed us
with new faith,
fertile from the Teller of parables.

Warm as the breath
of a loved one
whispering forgiveness
and unearned respect,
so your Spirit
breathes renovating grace
into our dispirited souls.

Some days you spin
like a willy-willy,
startling, tearing, hurting,
uprooting us from apathy
and leaving us giddy
with new possibilities
in discipleship.

Like a soft breeze at dusk
soothing tired faces
at the end of a hard day,
so you visit us
in the evening of life
when all our work is done,
giving us Christ's peace at the last.

We believe
in the Holy Spirit,
Lord, and giver of life,
Poured out on all flesh,
Who with the Father
and the Son,
is worshipped and glorified!
Amen!

Life in the Spirit

When earth was like a valley of skeletons,
　　you, wonderful God, came among us in power!
Your Jesus breathed on us and said:
　　'Receive the Holy Spirit'.
Like a mighty rushing wind:
　　'Receive the Holy Spirit'.
Like tongues of living fire:
　　'Receive the Holy Spirit'.
With love to the whole world:
　　'Receive the Holy Spirit'.

Lord, if we had not seen and heard,
　　we would not believe it;
That this valley of dry bones should live
　　is beyond our wildest expectations!
Yet now we hear rattling of bones
　　as dead and forgotten hopes reassemble;
We witness the astounding omen
　　of broken, impotent promises growing muscle;
Surprised, we watch old eye-sockets
　　filling with new and loving visions;
Cold arms pulse as with new blood,
　　embracing lonely and uncherished people;
Deadly-dull churchgoers stand tall
　　and celebrate the Gospel with style.
We see atrophied hands and feet inspired
　　to do the costly deeds of Jesus;
Bare bones, bleached by the winds of materialism,
　　become enfleshed with faith and love;
We hear voices, long ago incapable of blessing,
　　commence to sing the song of the angels.
Before our very eyes, unforgiving, bitter skeletons
　　begin to be merciful, even as our Father is merciful;
Grey, defeated forms, who despaired of any joy,
　　run and dance their way into the Kingdom!

Holy Spirit, Lord, and giver of life,
   praise belongs to you for ever!
The Gospel is announced to the poor:
   praise belongs to you for ever!
Release for prisoners, sight for the blind;
Yes, the time has come
   when the Lord will save his people:
   praise belongs to you for ever!

Our God

Your rainbow shines
   its hope across all lands:
Christ's new creation,
   grasped by loving hands.

You are the bridge
   which spans our separation;
Christ's life laid down
   the new foundation.

Your vast acceptance
   liberates from fear;
Christ's fellow-heirs
   high-spirited appear.

Full of surprises
   is Christ's God and ours;
the weak rejoice
   in unexpected powers.

Our roots grow deep,
   firm in the ground which holds us;
Christ's subtle strength
   where love enfolds us.

All Saints' Day

Psalm 94

Lord, you are a God of justice;
    show it to my countrymen!
Ruler of the whole cosmos,
    give the arrogant what they deserve!
How long is it going to go on, Lord —
    this insolence of heartless power-brokers?

Lord, it burns me up,
    the way weak people are exploited.
Aborigines have their sacred shrines despoiled,
    ravaged for mineral deposits.
Widows and migrants are sucked in,
    fooled by the fine print in hire-purchase agreements.
Grog and drugs are peddled to our youth,
    and they slaughter each other on the roads.

Yet, Lord, big business brags about it,
    publishing its profits in the financial pages.
Shareholders are sometimes demonic, Lord,
    when profits become the only value.
Ordinary people seem far removed,
    pawns without names or faces.
Our sophistical friends tell us not to worry;
    God doesn't care, so why should we?

Listen, you well-groomed dumb-heads!
    Suave fools, wake up to yourselves!
Does he who created ears hear no crying,
    the Lord who gave eyes see no suffering?
Can't he who instructs the nations give correction?
    Doesn't the teacher of mankind know anything?
The Lord knows our sophisticated minds;
    we are nothing but foul wind-bags!

Happiness is accepting the Lord's discipline,
    learning the ways of love;
Standing firm when all goes against you,
    until the wicked fall into their own pit.
The Lord will never abandon his people;
    he won't walk out on his own.
In the end, goodness will have its way;
    the future belongs to compassionate people.

Who will stand with me against apathy?
    Who sides with me against corruption?
If the Lord had not helped me,
    I would have been in the cemetery long ago!
When I find myself giving in,
    your love, Lord, holds me up.
When anxiety seizes my mind,
    your presence is my comfort and joy.

Lord, can corporate evil get your vote,
    or those who twist the law defeat us —
Those who slander good men as troublemakers
    and allow defenceless people to die?
No way! The Lord is utterly dependable;
    my God is more solid than granite.
In the Lord's own time they will fall;
    'respectable' crime will get what it deserves!

Australia Day

Psalm 136

Thank the Lord, the source of all goodness,
The True-God of True-God,
   His love endures for ever!
Thank the Ruler of all rulers,
Who alone achieves the impossible.
   His love endures for ever!

His wisdom made boundless galaxies,
He placed this planet in orbit,
And gave us lights to order our lives;
By day the sun, moon and stars by night.
   His love endures for ever!

Oppressors he has punished;
Pharaoh of old, and Hitler in our century.
His faithful people he has rescued:
Moses, Peter, Luther, Knox, and Niemoller.
   His love endures for ever!

He sailed with the convicts to Botany Bay,
Brought down unscrupulous governors,
Led settlers through alien bush,
And turned prisoners into free men.
   His love endures for ever!

He gave a homeland to unwanted people,
A rich heritage to those who serve him.
When we were under attack he remembered us,
Rescued us from those who sought to invade us.
   His love endures for ever!

Nor does the Lord forget his lowly creatures:
Platypus and pelican eat well.
He gives grass for the wallaroo and seeds for lorikeets;
He feeds the marsupial mouse and the echidna.
O give thanks to the God of every living thing!
   His love endures for ever!

Brisbane skyline.

Anzac Day

Psalm 90

Lord, the ages come and go,
    but you remain as our homing-point.
Before you gave birth to mountains,
    before the travail of this planet,
Back beyond the beginning,
    you have been God.

You return every person to dust,
    saying: 'Back you go, mortals'.
In your eyes a thousand years are like yesterday,
    or like an hour's sleep during the night.
You sweep people away like a flood;
    we are as grass in the early morning —
In the morning it bursts with green life,
    yet by evening it is cut and withered.
So are we consumed by your discipline,
    and by your power we are dismissed.
Our mistakes are naked before you,
    our guilty secrets are exposed to your glance.
Every day dissolves in your power;
    our life ends as suddenly as a short story.
We only live for about seventy years —
    if we are strong, perhaps eighty.
It is a span of struggle and grief;
    soon it is over and we take wing.
Yet do we make time to think of your discipline?
    And who gives respect equal to your power?

Please teach us to treasure every day,
    taking to heart your brand of wisdom.
Stand by us, Lord, through every long day;
    have pity on all your workers.
Fill us with your free love,
    so that we may laugh and sing.
Give us joy to match our daily grind,
    and happiness to mix with the years of pain.
Help your workers to see you at work among us,
    that our children may recognize your glory.
We want the beauty of our God to be upon us,
    till the works of our hands share your eternal purpose.

Church Anniversary

Enter these doors with thanksgiving,
   come into this sanctuary with praise;
Be grateful for the gift of the Church Universal,
   and praise the Lord for the church in this place.

For . . . years of continuous worship;
   for . . . years of sincere service;
     we thank you, O Lord.
For those who initiated this fellowship,
   and those who built this sanctuary:
     we thank you, O Lord.
For people who used their gifts of leadership,
   and people who gave loyalty and love:
     we thank you, O Lord.
For the Gospel proclaimed in this church,
   and the Gospel received within these walls:
     we thank you, O Lord.
For all who in sorrow found comfort,
   and all who in weakness found strength:
     we thank you, O Lord.
For the fellowship which has given support,
   and the fellowship which has challenged and disturbed:
     we thank you, O Lord.
For times when this church has been packed,
   and times when only a few have worshipped:
     we thank you, O Lord.
For the rich memories of years gone by,
   and the opportunities in years to come:
     we praise you, O Lord most High.

Your Church, O God, has embraced us;
   Its one loving Lord has redeemed us.
With all your people who ever were, are, or will be,
   we would worship and serve you for ever!

Come Quickly!

Psalm 63

My God in whom I trust,
    I look for your early coming.
Body and soul, I thirst for you
    like a man lost in the outback.
Through country and city I search for you,
    looking for signs of your glory.
Your love is dearer than life itself;
    my lips hunger for adequate praise.
As long as I live I'll serve you;
    my hands shall honour your name.

When you come I shall be satisfied,
    as a guest at a King's table.
I'll lie awake on my bed,
    marvelling at your hospitality.
For you are my only help;
    in your coming is true joy.
Willingly I'll be a disciple,
    your strong hand pointing the way.

The false goals that distract me
    shall crumble into the dust;
Everything that threatens my hope
    shall be as carrion for the crows.
All deceit shall be silenced
    when allegiance is sworn to you.
Let every ruler rejoice in you
    when you come to be our King!

Photo Credits

Page
11 Seals at Seal Bay, SA — Publicity and Design Services, Premier's Dpt, SA
15 Outback signposts — Dpt of Tourism, Qld
18 Fruitcart, Rundle Mall, Adelaide — Publicity and Design Services, Premier's Dpt, SA
22 Brushtailed possums — Dpt of Tourism, Qld
25 Wheatfields — WA Dpt of Tourism
30 Most s-w tip of Australia, Cape Leeuwin, WA — B.D. Prewer
35 Stand of wattles — WA Dpt of Tourism
41 Sydney Harbour and Opera House — Dpt of Tourism, NSW
45 Reflections, Wynyard Lake, Tas. — B.D. Prewer
52 Tanks and windmill — Dpt of Tourism, NSW
56 Ayers Rock — NT Tourist Board
62 Sheepshearing — Dpt of Tourism, NSW
66 The Nut, Stanley, Tas. — Dpt of Tourism, Tas.
67 Wave Rock, near Hyden, WA — WA Dpt of Tourism
75 Sunrise, Moralana Scenic Drive, SA — Publicity and Design Services, Premier's Dpt, SA
81 Mallacoota Beach, Vic. — B.D. Prewer
86 Nullarbor Highway — Publicity and Design Services, Premier's Dpt, SA
97 Senator Neville Bonner — N.T. Bonner
101 Sydney Domain — Dpt of Tourism, NSW
107 Crater Lake, Tas. — B.D. Prewer
113 Palm Sunday service of worship and witness, Mt Waverley, Vic., 1973 — B.D. Prewer
123 Brisbane skyline — Dpt of Tourism, Qld

Cover
The Red Cap Gum (Eucalyptus erythrocorys)

PART II

Australian Prayers

Australian Prayers

has been reproduced
from the seventh printing of the
1983 Lutheran Publishing House Edition.

To my oldest friends:
Cliff and Florrie

INTRODUCTION

*'In your prayers do not go babbling on like the heathen,
who imagine that the more they say the more likely they
are to be heard.'*

Having compiled this volume of original prayers, I have become
more aware of the warning which Jesus gave concerning wordy and
repetitious praying.

This collection is gleaned from the last four years of my service as
an ordained minister within the church. About eighty per cent are
prayers which were composed for particular congregations at
particular times. The remainder are some of my own private prayers,
formed during times of meditation, either in the parish setting or
during normal periods of leave.

In my opening sentence above, I used the word 'original'. That is a
foolish word to use. Some wise person has said: 'The art of
originality is forgetting where one first read it.' That must be true in
this case. I am indebted to thousands of people who have shared
their prayers, either in worship beside me, or within books. Also I
have been seeded with the great prayers of the ages, especially
those of the Jewish and Christian traditions. Even beyond that, there
have been times of awareness when I knew my praying has been
God praying through me, as the 'groans of the Spirit' pleaded from
within me. At the end of this complex process, these particular
prayers have emerged with the stamp of my faith and personality on
them. Only in this sense are they original.

They are called 'Australian Prayers'. This is not to claim that they
draw exclusively on the idiom and imagery of Australia. Some are, in
fact, more colourfully Australian than others; but most are simply
the prayers of one Australian praying among other Australians. Do
not expect, or fear, that you will discover kangaroos and banksia
trees waltzing through every page.

There is little that is unique or special about this collection. It is not presented to surprise, shock, or impress. Although unassuming, I hope the prayers avoid both the jargon of academic theology and that cheap, 'folksy' language which has more in common with the prattle of football commentators than holy dialogue. They are simply the record of real praying that happened among God's people; no more than that.

Those confessions, joys, pleadings, and aspirations have now become little symbols printed on paper which have no breath of their own, and may mean little or nothing. This is good. My efforts are reduced to a sane size. Whether they live again is entirely beyond my power. So I am led back to the crux of things: that grace which alone can give new life to one single phrase.

Bruce Prewer,
Pilgrim Church, Adelaide

Easter 1983

CONTENTS

Part I: ADVANCE AUSTRALIA
Days, Places, and Moods

Australia Day 10
Anzac Day 11
Labour Day 12
New Year's Eve 14
Loving This Continent 16
Wilderness 17
Murray Matins 18
Vespers by the Murray River 20
Huon Pine 22
Canberra 23

Song of the Jarrah 24
Ancient Gumtrees 25
God of Winter 26
An Evening in Autumn 27
Signs of Grace in Springtime 28
Without You, Life is Desert 29
Lament for My People 30
As Raucous as the Wattle Bird 31
Such a Strange Mixture 32

Part II: WHEN IT'S IN SEASON
Events in the Church Calendar

Preparation 36
Wake Us from Slumber and Apathy 36
Come, Advent God 38
Christmas Confession 39
Emmanuel 40
Remembering the Needy at Christmas 41
Contradictions 42
Searching and Finding 43
On Transfiguration Day 44
Lent 45
Palm Sunday 46
He Who Comes 47
The Suffering Servant 48

Behold the Man 50
Good Friday Intercessions 52
Easter 54
Easter Mercies 56
The Right-Hand Man 58
City Pentecost 59
Pentecost Confession 60
Spirit 61
Holy Spirit, Help Us 62
Trinity 63
All Souls 64
Our Paradox King 66

Part III: SMALL IS BEAUTIFUL
Collects on Various Themes

On Fieldlarks' Wings 70
On the Rays of the Morning 70
Trusting New Life 70
Twentieth-Century Saints 71
As Eagle and Dolphin 71
Daybreak 71
Touch and Heal Us 72
Like a Plover 73
For Lightweights 73

Divine Generosity 73
Morning 74
The Word and the Babble 74
Unspeakable Joys 74
Needed Gifts 75
Listen to Our Brother 75
Reedwarbler 76
God of the Evening 76
Joy on Grey Days 76

Bonuses 77
When Honour Departs 78
A Quiet Spirit 78
Victorious................................ 78
Endings and Beginnings 79
This New Day 79

Incarnation 80
Hearing the Angels' Song 80
Christ the King 81
Advent 81
Partners in Love 82
Good Shepherd........................ 82

Part IV: GO IN PEACE
Confession and Forgiveness

Shame and Glory...................... 84
To Be More Loving 85
Losing Faith 86
When We Fail to Love 87
Failure to Love 88
Faith and Works 89
To Know Ourselves................... 90

Hurry and Worry 91
Lost in the Traffic 92
Double Standards 92
Judge Not 93
For Recovery of Joy and Liberty .. 94
Bring Us to Our Senses............. 95

Part V: GOOD TO BE ALIVE
Thanksgiving and Praise

Full of Grace and Truth 98
Gloria in Excelsis 100
The Name: Jesus 101
Endless Love 102
Focus 103
Baptized by the Morning 104
Great Thanksgiving 105
Thanksgiving for Light 106

Evening Prayer 107
Good to be Alive......................108
For Faith 110
Good Morning..........................111
Special People..........................112
A Child's Gratitude 113
Springtime...............................114
For All His Mercies 116

Part VI: LOVE YOUR NEIGHBOUR
Sharing the Concerns of the Lord

Inasmuch 118
Where People Live....................119
Transforming Misfortunes 120
Our City 121
Strengthen Our Resolve.............122
Our Black People 122
Planting True Vines...................124
For Church and World 125
For Those who Hunger 126

The Way of Truth 128
Entertainers 129
Shepherd of Your Sheep............130
Itinerant Workers 130
Small Country Towns 132
Children in Hospital...................133
Bushfires 134
Forgotten People 136

Part VII: AS YOU LOVE YOURSELF
Be with us Lord

Today in the City 138
Hallowed be Your Name 138
In Spirit and Truth 139
Long Weekend 140
Turn to Us 142
Save Your Children 144
Shepherd Us 145

All who are Heavy Laden 146
Be with Us 147
Peace of God 148
For Deliverance 148
Contemporary Wilderness 150
Light 151
Renew Our Spirit 152

Part VIII: FOR SHEPHERDS ONLY
Ministers, Pastors and Priests

New in the Parish 154
Serving at Table 155
Our Peculiar Temptations 156
Enigma 157

Bitter Cup 158
One Minute before the Sermon .. 159

Photo Credits 160

Part I

ADVANCE AUSTRALIA
Days, Places, and Moods

Australia Day

God of Australia, you have loved this ancient land
long before human eye explored it. On this Australia Day
we offer mixed feelings of praise and plea for our nation.

We bring you our gratitude
for the diversity and wealth
of this land and its people:
for its weathered old mountains, fertile valleys,
and vast plains;
for its riches of mine and agriculture,
forest, and grazing lands;
for our black people who know and love this continent
with an intimate, profound sensitivity;
for the courage, vision, and sacrifice of the early settlers;
for the diverse races who now call Australia home:
For these and all your gifts
we offer you, O Lord, our joyful, thankful hearts.

We also bring confession
of the evil
which has marred our country
and injured our citizens:
for the rapacious way we have exploited the good earth
for quick monetary gain, with little thought for the future;
for the ugliness we have imposed on places of rare beauty
through our vandalism — both legal and illegal;
for our history of vile inhumanity
toward our black sisters and brothers,
and for the injustices which they still suffer;
for our neglect of minority groups and our continuing
racist intolerance toward some immigrants;
for our blatant selfishness which has helped
create and maintain the caste of the unemployed:

Have mercy upon us, O God.
Bring us to repentance.
Forgive and renew us
with the grace of our Lord Jesus Christ.

God, our God,
take us all and lead our nation
toward the higher destiny
which belongs to the children of God:
through Jesus, our First Citizen and Lord.

Anzac Day

God of the living and the dead,
console and encourage
those for whom this day
is one of profound significance.

Be with the widows,
spinsters, orphans and the totally disabled,
who together with the dear and honoured dead
have sacrificed so much.
By your grace,
work in the hearts and minds of men and women
who today are reliving
the agony, courage, and compassion
of war service.

Help all of us to honour
those who have made so great a sacrifice,
yet save us
from ever glorifying the evil of war.
Enable us to be peacemakers.
Hasten the great day
when nation shall not lift up sword against nation,
neither shall they learn war any more.

This we pray
in the name of the One who sacrificed his all
for the sake of the world:
Jesus Christ, our Redeemer and Lord.

Labour Day

God of the Carpenter,
we thank you for this day
on which we can celebrate
the value of all who labour
in the basic tasks of our community.

For the efforts
of all those who in recent centuries
have fought for the dignity
and rights of all workers:
We thank you, God of the Carpenter.

For the upgrading
of working conditions, safety precautions,
the length of work-hours,
and justified wages:
We thank you, God of the Carpenter.

For the gift of those
who do the dirtiest jobs,
who have the most boring tasks,
or who are still exposed to dangers:
We thank you, God of the Carpenter.

For all whose health has suffered,
For the weary who don't know how to keep going,
and the weak whose strength is failing:
We pray to you, O Lord.

For all who are still exploited,
especially migrants and women;
For those who are victimized by foremen,
and those who must work beside ugly characters:
We pray to you, O Lord.

For those who do work which is degrading,
people who feel compromised and dishonest,
workers who suffer sexual harassment,
those who have no friends among fellow-workers,
and all who have been demoted at work:
We pray to you, O Lord.

For the many who have recently been sacked,
the thousands who have been unemployed for years;
for the families of the unemployed who are suffering,
and those without work who are tempted to turn to crime;
for the young who feel hopeless about the future,
and the middle-aged who feel useless:
We pray to you, O Lord.

Father of Jesus,
God of all workers,
bless your people
and lead us all
to that time when the workers of this world
may be treated
with justice and respect:
through Jesus Christ, the worker from Nazareth.

New Year's Eve

Lord of all our days,
be with us tonight,
when the car horns hoot,
church bells ring,
crowds shout and cheer,
and 'Auld Lang Syne'
is sung at numerous parties.

Let those of us who love you
celebrate with as much joy
but with more purpose than
those who love you not.

Put a new song of faith
on our lips,
and renew the optimism of grace
within our mind and heart:
through Christ our Lord.

*   *   *

God of the old year
which is passing away,
we commend to your mercy
those who are glad to finish this year.

We lift up before you
those who have critically overworked,
those who had no opportunity to work,
folk whose health has broken up,
or whose career has been shattered;
our neighbours who have tasted grief,
or who have contracted terminal illness;
people who will end this year homeless,
and those who end it in hunger or thirst.

*   *   *

God of the new year
which is dawning,
we also commend to your mercy
those who enter the new year eagerly.

We hold up before you
all who will take up new work,
or who will retire from work;
all who plan to be married,
or who look forward to parenthood;
the people who will buy their own home,
or who will commence at universities;
those who will come to faith in you,
and all whose faith will grow stronger.

God of the past, present
and the limitless future,
bless all your people,
that, set free from old fears
or shallow optimism,
we may live with the joy
of the children of God.

Loving This Continent

Source of all love and joy,
Father of Jesus and our God,
to you belongs our gratitude.
Your loyalty to us is untiring
and your love is beyond all measure.
We thank you, Lord of Life.

When our continent was being created
you thought of us and provided for us.
When our land's inhabitants
were kangaroo and koala,
jabiru and carrawong,
alligator and yabbie,
you catered for our needs.
We thank you, Lord of Life.

When we inherited this land,
we used it recklessly and selfishly,
but you did not give us up.
Though, like tramps, we wander among our broken promises,
shattered hopes, and empty prayers,
you give us Jesus the Christ,
to seek and save the lost.
We thank you, Lord of Life.

Though Australians become blinded by technology,
misled by opinion-poll morality,
hardened by greed, and captivated by lusts,
through Jesus Christ you still come among us
inviting us to reclaim our destiny
as your very children.
We thank you, Lord of Life.

God of Jesus,
God of the Southern Cross
and of all who read its sign,
make our nation your nation.
Let us live to your glory,
today
and as long as this land shall last.

Wilderness

The wilderness and the dry land shall be glad,
the desert shall rejoice and blossom.
In solitary places praises rise,
when we are glad for the wilderness.

For the Coorong, with its sand dunes,
waterways and pelican,
the Flinders' flocks of emu
among the daisy plains,
the cedars of New England,
the flame tree, and creepers:
We thank you, God of the wilderness.

For Russell Falls and Franklin gorges,
the grandeur of the Inland,
and the mysteries of Ayers Rock,
the jagged peaks of Stirling Ranges
and their slopes spread with flowers:
We thank you, God of the wilderness.

For the velvet woodlands of the Conway
and the fossicking of brush turkeys,
the heathlands of Yanchep
and black swans by the lake,
the volcanic spires of Warrambungle
and the sungolds ablaze:
We thank you, God of the wilderness.

For Lamington Plateau
with its jungle and paddy-melons,
the screech of cockatoos
among the Grampians' buttresses,
the host of ferns, palms, and mosses
in the oasis of Palm Valley:
We thank you, God of the wilderness

For the bliss of being awed by ancient beauty,
for new perspective given to harassed lives,
for the gift of solitude in the presence of the elemental:
We thank you, God of the wilderness.

Murray River Matins

Communing Spirit,
you share with me
the profound loveliness
of this soft, grey morning
in the stillness of the bush
beside this wide water
which reflects
like glazed ceramic
the sentinel river gums.

Early you watched with me
the approach of the faithful old sun,
which from below the wide horizon
threw shafts of salmon light
upon the low cloud banks,
and deftly tinted
the sleepy face of the creek.

Beside me,
yet through me,
you, most intimate Spirit,
have pleasured intensely
in the seried flights of pelicans
returning from a night's fishing,
gliding authoritatively between
an avenue of gum trees
to take their morning rest
among the feathered tribe
which dozes noiselessly
by a sheltered billabong.

Through my ears
you have listened
to the egret's squawk
as it tries out roosting places
on half-submerged bare tree limbs.
You hear the mournful cry
of the ubiquitous black crow,
the chatter of lorikeets,
and, in between these,
the rare sound of silence.

You, Agape Spirit,
have communed with me
on this gentle morning,
infilling my life with something
of your elemental serenity,
awakening an awe which leavens
the supreme contentment of wholeness,
yet leaves me raw
and more exposed
to threats of existence.

Creator Spirit,
like your Jesus
help me increasingly
to trust your serene communion,
and like Jesus,
when it is needed,
to accept the holy way
of the cross which weighs
so painfully on souls
made sensitive to beauty.

Vespers by the Murray River

The winter sun
finds a gap in sombre clouds
through which to project
its last strong strands of golden light
across the wide old river,
and among the piebald
trunks of river gums,
then plays briefly on the face
of distant red-clay cliffs.

Old man Murray
flows by almost imperceptibly,
silently making pilgrimage
toward his destiny
in the Southern Ocean.
No winds disturb his peace;
and so, gently smiling,
he mirrors the evening shapes,
and tempts a redfin
to leap three times
in spasms of joy.

A grey heron,
its yellow legs knee-deep,
wades with ballerina delicacy
along the river's flank.
A pure white egret
patiently stands statuesque,
its perfect reflection
like a Siamese twin
looks up at it from the water.
Then a flotilla of pelicans
glides effortlessly by with the dignity
of stately galleons
from some bygone age.

All is still and gentle
as if all creation shares
with tender empathy
the last whisper
of this dying day.
The lights are low now,
and everything is suspended
as if waiting
for some final word.

Then without warning,
with no introit,
God's cheerful choristers
the kookaburras
dent the evening air
with the joyful vesper
which has been sung
across our motherland
from time immemorial.

And I, a late migrant
to this scheme of things,
feel my spirit leap within me
to share this ancient canticle
of gratitude and joy.

Lord, now let your servant
lie down in peace this night;
and, if it pleases you,
let me wake tomorrow
to the song of your glad choir
among these aged gums,
chanting a jubilant sanctus
for the gift of a new day.

Huon Pine

Lord, how I enjoy
the aroma and feel
of this timber of yours
which spins
on my wood-lathe
like a prayer-wheel.

Here, revealing to me
its texture,
are a thousand years
of growth and setback
in the rain forests
of the Franklin.

Here is the nurture
of a Creator
who is not in a hurry
to achieve
things of rare beauty
and utility.

A millennium of seasons
coded here
in the fine grain:
torrential rains, blankets of snow,
and the energy of the sun
in a thousand Springtimes.

How many times
did this fragment of creation
vibrate with birdsong,
the growl of Tasmanian tiger,
or the chant and dance
of early Aborigines?

What deep secrets
does it hide
as I attempt
to plane and polish it
into new patterns
of beauty?

As I touch this texture,
grant me the sensitivity
to learn from this Huon Pine
yet another parable
of the Creator's
joy and pain.

Canberra

God of the 'City Splendid',
we pray for our Federal Capital of Canberra:

city of superb planning and of high hopes,
city of noble architecture and national treasures,
city of politicians, public servants, and tourists,
of university, Mint, and embassies,
of growing churches, families, and schools;

city of endeavour and much frustration,
of tarnished ideals and crumbling hopes,
of intrigue, rumour, and cynicism,
city of weary public servants,
the coliseum of those hungry for power,
the cemetery of fallen idols
and broken idealists.

In your great wisdom and mercy, Lord,
forgive and bless your city of Canberra.

Song of the Jarrah

Master,
incomparable woodturner,
you take tough jarrah
    like me,
    and from it
fashion things more beautiful
    than eye has seen
    or ear heard.

Some days
you uncover in me
    a grain-pattern
    fine and elegant
which I never knew
    I possessed.

Sometimes
you work patiently
    through sapholes
    knots, or rogue grain,
spinning contours of grace
    in spite of all.

Carpenter,
irrepressible craftsman,
you even became jarrah
    in the lathe
    in order to share
    the pain of the mis-shapen,
    the joy of the new-shaped,
and the love song
    of jarrah's Creator.

Ancient Gumtrees

Lord, your ancient, noble red gums
    scattered across the grass lands
    of southern plain and valleys,
never fail to move me,
awakening a mood
of admiration, awe,
and meditation.

Their weathered, warped limbs,
    gnarled and distorted
    like the arthritic limbs,
    hands and fingers,
    of one most dear to me,
insist on reaching
out and up
in some defiant ballet
of divine celebration.

Immense trunks,
    bent in a long-past
    sapling-youth
    by prevailing winds,
    and scarred from storms
    which centuries ago
    tore out limbs,
invite me to touch
and gently feel the texture,
or rest my cheek
in love.

Fed by massive, mis-shapen roots
    which, before my life began,
    had already explored
    the ground of their being
    and found it sufficient,
these old folk, Lord,
of your other kingdom,
share with me
the secret of grace.

God of Winter

God of winter,
we praise you:
God of soaking rains,
of hail and snow, wind and storm,
of torrents surging down creek beds,
streams filling reservoirs,
and tanks full and running over.

God of brisk winter mornings,
of frosted paddocks under moonlight,
of warm socks, coats, and gloves,
heaters, radiators, and glowing fires.

God of birds singing eagerly
when the gentle sun breaks through clouds,
of mallee trees tipped with new growth,
and wattles budding, eager for spring.

God of stark hillsides,
clothed for a season in soft green,
and of moist cultivated wheatfields,
where tractors work long into night.

God of little children splashing in puddles,
sailing make-believe boats in flooded gutters,
of raincoats, and umbrellas, and gum-boots,
and the scent of hot soup from the kitchen.

God of winter, glorious winter,
the unpopular, slandered season,
yet one filled with renewed hope
for farms, town, and city.

God of life-sustaining winter,
author of re-creation and providence
renewing the roots of life,
God of glorious winter,
blessed is your name
in all the earth!

An Evening in Autumn

Blessed be your name, O most blessed giver of seasons.
This autumn evening is your gift;
    the gentle air caresses our faces,
    the scent of soil after rain
    is fragrant in our nostrils,
    the body relaxes,
    and the mind absorbs the quiet of dusk.
The meal time is over,
    children have ceased their games and gone inside,
    and the birds have ended their songs —
except for the evening call
of a lone wagtail from a jacaranda tree.
Above and beyond our planet,
the velvet flanks of space
    begin to glisten with the light of stars
supported by a thin crescent of light from a young moon.

This evening, Lord,
our praise rises as simply and sweetly
as the call of that lone wagtail.

'It is good to give thanks to the Lord,
to sing songs of your love, Most loving One!
To affirm your presence in the morning,
and at evening to sing of your love,
to pluck the strings of the guitar,
to give melody to the flute
and make harmony on the harp.
Your deeds, O Lord, fill me with gladness;
your gifts move me to songs of joy.'
Hallelujah!

Signs of Grace in Springtime

Our Father in Jesus and our God,
earth and sky,
sunshine and rain,
tree and flower,
speak to us of your creative power.
Lord, open our eyes to see your beauty.

The sheep on the plains,
the cattle on the hills,
the fish of the sea,
and the birds of the air,
tell of your bountiful providence.
Lord, open our hearts to experience your goodness.

The jacaranda bursts into flower
with a robe of royal beauty —
a symbol of Christ our Redeemer,
of glory he alone is fit to wear.
Lord, you are the King of love, and we are your people.

The lush greening of the vines
reminds us of Jesus, the True Vine,
in whom we must abide
if we are to bear fruit.
Lord, you are the Vine, and we are the branches.

The crimson bottlebrush
witnesses to the blood of the cross,
the cost of our salvation,
and the wonder of forgiveness.
*Lord, your mercy makes all things new;
we open our lives to your grace.*

The singing of the birds
at dawn and dusk
awaken within us the melodies of
faith, hope, and love,
stirring a hunger for the world-wide harmony
and peace which you have promised.
Lord, we thank you,
we trust you,
we love you,
we praise you,
and we worship your name,
world without end.

Without You, Life Is Desert

God, how we need your help!
Without you, life is like the Stony Desert;
with you, life is like the Channel Country
after abundant rains.

If we have become bare and unfruitful,
like a neglected paddock,
be to us as a plough in hard ground.

If we have wandered in waste places,
becoming lost and blinded in sandstorms,
lead us to some quiet, verdant gully,
where there is living water to refresh us,
soft ferns to caress our tiredness away,
and sweet rest on the mossy bank
of your grace, mercy, and peace.

God, how we need your help!
If we are to live fruitfully,
and love our fellows with a love like yours,
we need you every hour!

Lament for My People

Lord, my people have become mopokes,
enjoying the darkness,
but blind in the light.
Where is Australia going, Lord?
Is there any hope for this people
that I dearly love?

What will become of a people
whose gambling bill far outstrips
all pensions to the needy —
who feed rump steak to greyhounds,
and do not notice unemployed citizens
sorting through rubbish bins?

Is there any future for a people
who spend a thousand times more
on assorted pet foods
than they give to the starving
people in our cruel world?

What will become of a society
where married couples
prefer pets and yearly travel
to the joys and disciplines
of family love?

Can we survive as a nation
when, before every election,
our first question is:
'What is in it for me?'

Lord, have mercy.
Christ, have mercy.
Lord, have mercy.
And save us all.

Speak your word of judgment and mercy
to me — and to all my fellow-Australians.
For my people are your people, Lord,
and you understand them
and love them more profoundly
than I ever can.
Lord, when we burrow like wombats to evade you,
deal with us with strong discipline;
make us face the truth,
and live by the light that shines
in Jesus Christ our Lord.

As Raucous as the Wattle Bird

As the raucous cry of the wattle bird
sounds from among fresh gum blossom,
so must my discordant praise sound
in your ears,
my love, my life, my Lord!

Yet you know that my prayer is true,
that my songs of joy are the sweetest melodies
that my heart can compose.

If there is singing among the holy angels
when lost coins and sheep are found,
and when lost children return home,

there is also great joy
among the lost things of this earth
when we, who are found, discover
that you have made a home with us,

and that heaven and earth are becoming one
through Jesus Christ our Lord.

Jubilate Deo!
My love, my life, my Lord!

Such a Strange Mixture

I'm such a strange mixture, Lord;
something greater than human wisdom
      is needed to sort me out
      and make me whole.

Some days I soar like an eagle
      over the peaks of the Great Divide;
Yet on other days I'm like a cockroach
      hiding in dark places.

Sometimes, like a surfer at Coolangatta,
      I truly enjoy riding life's rough waves;
But at other times I just sit and complain,
      allowing the surf to break over me,
      filling my eyes with grit
      and my soul with self-pity.

There are special moments of prayer
      when I beg you to take me hiking
      among the mountain-places of the Spirit —
Followed by pessimistic moods
      when my bleating prayers
      rise no higher than ant hills.

Lord, you have searched me and known me.
You know the strange mixture
      that hides behind my public face.
Take me in hand.
Be to me not the God I want,
      But the God I need.

Part II

WHEN IT'S IN SEASON
Events in the Church Calendar

Preparation

This is the season of His coming;
Night is far gone, the day is at hand.

It is time to wake from sleep;
*For the Son of Man comes at an hour
we do not expect.*

His coming is the advent of saving love.
Come, Lord Jesus.

His coming is good news for the poor,
freedom for captives, sight for the blind,
liberty for the oppressed,
and acceptance for the unacceptable.
Come, Lord Jesus.

Then shall the lame man leap like the hart,
and the tongue of the dumb sing for joy.
O come, O come, Immanuel.

Wake Us from Slumber and Apathy

Advent God,
awaken us from our slumber,
shock us out of our apathy.

Come to us
    like the thunder of the surf
    pounding Bell's Beach,
    like the mighty roar of the wind
    surging through blue gum forests.

Come to us
  with whatever shock
  or discipline is needed
  to awaken drowsy disciples.

For the night is far spent,
the dawn is at hand,
and now is our salvation nearer
than when we first believed.

Come, O come, Immanuel,
save your Australian people;
confront us afresh
until all hearts are full
of the Word made flesh.

Advent God,
we praise you!
Glory to the One who comes
in the name of the Lord!
Hallelujah!

Come, Advent God

Come, Advent God,
and complete the special work of love
which you began in Jesus of Nazareth.

Many are cast down with spiritual needs,
thirsting for the peace of your forgiveness
and the warmth of your healing love.
Come to them with the grace they desperately need.
At evening or midnight, morning or midday,
Come, Lord Jesus.

Many are in despair through physical hardship,
seeking relief from their burdens
and hope in the midst of their cares.
Come to them with the help they desperately need.
At evening or midnight, morning or midday,
Come, Lord Jesus.

Many have minds and souls filled with hatred,
lives shackled by prejudice and terrible obsession
in Northern Ireland, the Middle East, Africa,
South America, Asia, and in our own Australia.
Come to them with the conversion they so desperately need.
At evening or midnight, morning or midday,
Come, Lord Jesus.

Your church in all the world also needs saving
from everything that threatens its mission.
Where it is persecuted, keep it faithful.
Where it persecutes, rebuke it.
Where it is seduced by affluence, shake it to its foundations.
Where it is self-satisfied, thoroughly unsettle it.
Where it is weak, poor, and meek, bless it with your joy, peace
and strength.
At evening or midnight, morning or midday,
Come, Lord Jesus.

Come, Advent God,
and complete your work in Jesus Christ,
through whom we offer these prayers.

Christmas Confession

If we have arrived at a time in our lives
when the Christmas story no longer
excites or renews us:
Have mercy upon us, O God.

If, in the midst of the riches of the Gospel
of Jesus Christ, we live like paupers:
Have mercy upon us, O God.

If the life of Jesus fails to challenge us,
or his death and resurrection cease to comfort us:
Have mercy upon us, O God.

If, in the face of the world's great need,
we hoard the Gospel like misers:
Have mercy upon us, O God.

(Silent meditation)

So that we may be forgiven and renewed:
Restore to us the joy of salvation.

So that we may be a loving community:
Restore to us the joy of salvation.

So that we may clothe our good intentions
with the garments of action:
*Restore to us the joy of your salvation,
through Jesus Christ our Lord.*

Emmanuel

God, in your grace and mercy,
you gave us your Son to be our Emmanuel;
give us a renewal of faith and life at this Christmas time,
and save us from our myths and evasions.

When we trivialize the Christmas Gospel:
Lord, have mercy.
When we talk of peace and goodwill,
with so little of it in our own lives:
Lord, have mercy.
So that we may not only sing carols and light candles,
but also serve the Christ
and allow the light to shine in and through us:
Lord, have mercy.

We thank you,
most generous God,
for all the peace and joy
which you give us.
We thank you
for sins forgiven,
hope renewed,
relationships repaired,
faith rekindled,
for your great love in Jesus Christ
established once again in our lives.

Jesus, our Emmanuel,
God with us,
we worship you
and joyfully offer the praise
of heart, voice, mind, and strength.

Remembering the Needy at Christmas

Lord, on this wonderful day we pause
to remember the needy people of this world
whom Jesus came to save:
May the light of his star touch every dark place.

As we meet in fellowship and goodwill,
we pray for the end of war and terrorism
in your torn world, especially ...
As we eat, drink, and are merry,
we pray for the hungry, homeless, and diseased:
Bring them your compassion and justice, Lord.

As we enjoy being relaxed and happy today,
we remember the sick,
the lonely, the frightened,
the anxious and the sorrowing:
Bring them your comfort and peace, Lord.

As we prepare to leave this place of prayer
to go our separate ways,
we remember those friends and loved ones
who are not with us this Christmas:
Give them the assurance of your presence, Lord.

As we pass other churches,
we remember other denominations,
praying especially for those
we fail to understand or appreciate:
Fill them with Christmas joy and praise, Lord.

O Word made flesh,
give us the will and capacity
to embody our prayers
in compassionate and courageous deeds:
Fill us with the joy of service.

God in the highest, worthy of glory,
hasten the day
when the song of the angels shall find perfect fulfilment:
In the name of your incarnate Son, Jesus.

Contradictions

God of vast generosity,
  your love planned the birth of the Baby
  who is born to save his people from their sins:

We confess to you and to each other,
  that, in this world of contradictions,
  we stand in need of your saving.

Forgive us
  if in the Christmas season we have used holy words
  in a shallow way,
  if we have conducted hollow celebrations,
  if we have given gifts only to those who give to us.

Forgive us
  if we have feasted without thanksgiving,
  caroled without joy,
  greeted without caring,
  and prayed without love.

May the living Word which has come to us —
  Emmanuel who is with us,
  Elder Brother who is one of us —
save us from our sins,
quieten us with his peace,
and fill us with his Spirit.

We delight to call his name Jesus,
for he is saving us from our sins.

Searching and Finding

Most loving God,
   who put it into the mind of the Wise Men
   to search for Jesus,
please give to us the wisdom to seek and to find.

When we become proud and stubborn,
give us the wisdom to find our humble Lord,
born in a stable.

When we become bewildered and lost in life's rush,
give us the wisdom to find ourselves
in the light that streams from Bethlehem.

When we become selfish and covetous,
cluttering our lives with possessions,
give us the wisdom to find that the best joy lies
in offering our treasures to Christ.

When we become depressed by our human failures and sin,
give us the wisdom to find the divine compassion and mercy,
the forgiveness which Jesus came to bring,
enabling us to name him Saviour from personal experience.

God of the Wise Men and our God,
put into our minds the wisdom
   to follow the star which leads us to Jesus Christ,
and to follow him, come what may,
   till our travelling days are done
and you call us home.

On Transfiguration Day

God of the transfigured Christ,
in your mercy transfigure us
and the whole world,
till the glory of Christ is seen
in the most unexpected places.

Transfigure our schools,
universities, medical schools,
and military colleges.

Transfigure our hospital wards,
our foster homes,
and our funeral parlours.

Transfigure our politics,
business and industry,
our laws and lawcourts.

Transfigure our friendships,
marriages, neighbourhood,
and all places of work.

Transfigure our charities,
overseas aid programs,
our refugee procedures and hostels.

Transfigure the church universal,
the churches of ...
and this congregation at ...,
as we meet for worship and service.

And in your boundless grace, O God,
transfigure our own
personal faith, hope, and love.

Lord of the mountain and plain,
of vision and sacrifice,
let us live in the light
and glory of your love
today and for ever:
through Jesus Christ our Lord.

Lent

O come, let us return unto the Lord:
For he will have mercy and abundantly pardon.
The Kingdom of heaven is at hand;
repent and believe the Gospel:
His will is our peace.
His discipline is our hope.
His service is perfect freedom.
In his presence is fullness of joy.

You cannot live by bread alone:
Lord, have mercy.
You shall not test the Lord your God:
Christ, have mercy.
You shall worship the Lord God,
and him only shall you serve:
Lord, have mercy.

O God, we are so immersed in the materialism of our age
that we find it hard to recognize our sins:
Open our eyes to see ourselves as you see us.
Expose the secret gods within us,
pinpoint the deceits that blur our perception,
unmask the poverty of our souls,
expose our greed, arrogance, or apathy,
save us from our love of things and use of persons,
deliver us from morbid guilt, cheap discipleship,
and sentimental religion:
through Jesus Christ who suffered and died for us.

Palm Sunday

Most loving God,
we confess that we are in danger
of making Palm Sunday a ceremony
rather than allowing it
to be an event in our lives.
Lord, have mercy:
Lord, have mercy.

If we sing our hosannas
within the safety of the church,
but rarely in public life,
Christ, have mercy:
Christ, have mercy.

So that our timidity may be transformed into courage,
and our indifference turned into costly love,
Lord, have mercy:
Lord, have mercy.

(Silent meditation)

Lord, have mercy upon us;
Christ, have mercy upon us,
Lord, have mercy upon us.

We thank you, O God, for Christ Jesus:
the word of forgiveness, the gospel of hope,
and the grace of new creation:
Hosanna! Blessed be the one who comes
in the name of the Lord.

We are grateful for the assurance
that Christ Jesus came into the world to save sinners:
Hosanna! Blessed be the one who comes
in the name of the Lord.
Hosanna in the highest!

He Who Comes

Hosanna! Blessed be the King who comes in the name of the Lord:
Hosanna in the highest!
If we should hold our peace, the very stones would shout aloud:
Hosanna in the highest!

God of the King
   who humbly rides on a donkey,
we who are conceited about our image and status,
   need your salvation:
Come, Lord, save us.
God of the pilgrims
   who publicly confessed their enthusiasm for Jesus,
we, who are embarrassed by public displays of faith,
   need your salvation:
Come, Lord, save us.
God of the hesitant
   who watched the holy procession,
   but were in two minds about joining it,
we, who often falter in our convictions,
   need your salvation:
Come, Lord, save us.

Gracious God, we thank you
for the experience of forgiveness
and the sense of your presence:
We praise your grace in Jesus Christ,
who makes disciples out of sinners,
and creates new life in tired or barren lives.

Hosanna! Blessed be the mercy
which comes in the name of the Lord:
Hosanna in the highest!

The Suffering Servant

O Lord, our Lord,
we have heard the most unlikely story;
we have seen your saving power in a weak Man.

He grew up quietly like a lonely plant,
    rooted in arid ground.
There was nothing to make one notice him,
    no good looks to impress the crowd.
His people despised and rejected him;
    a suffering, pathetic, neglected creature,
from him most turned their faces,
    reckoning him as useless.

Yet, unlike anyone else, he bore our lot,
    and carried the full ballast of our sorrows;
but we carried on as if he deserved his fate,
    sentenced to misery by God.
The wounds he bore were for our faults,
    the crown he wore was for our violations;
He suffered shame to bring us peace,
    tasted pain that we might be healed.

We are as stupid as sheep,
    wandering and lost;
but in and through this Man
    you have carried our shame.
His rights were openly violated
    yet he took it without complaint —
like a ewe before drunk shearers,
    as a lamb led to slaughter.

From the land of the living he was cut off;
    by our sins he was struck down.
Though he was never a violent man,
    nor ever spoke a treacherous word,
he died between criminals,
    and was buried in a borrowed grave.

Yet You did not forsake this bruised servant;
   you made his death the unique death,
and did the most unexpected thing:
   He rose to life again!
After the agony came light;
   after disgrace came vindication:
victory for himself and for others,
   banishing the burden of human disgrace.

Therefore this weak Man is for ever strong;
   His is the only, truly successful life.
He willingly staked his existence on you,
   and allowed himself to seem useless.
But, in fact, he bore our uselessness,
   and removed all charges against us.
His incomparable love-offering
   has become our true peace.

Behold The Man

Holy God,
this is the day
we most love,
yet hold in most awe.
We behold the Man,
and tremble.

O God,
as Jesus is lifted up,
our faith must either
be renewed or lost.
We see Him
and recognize
the kind of person
we want, yet are afraid, to be.

Behold the Man,
despised
outcast
accursed —
quite dispensable
when the powerful
snap their fingers
or rattle their money-bags.

God, we confess that
the things we deeply fear
meet us at this execution.
It is a nightmare,
from which we wish
to hide our faces:
from the One who seems abandoned
by earth and heaven.

This Golgotha is the place
where our smooth, sensible ideas of
success
power
wisdom
faith
and divine love
are shattered by a hammer beat.

Either we must abandon
this world's wisdom
and begin again,
or we must abandon
You, God.
Here at this Cross
our faith either rises
or falls.

Lord we believe,
Help us in our unbelief.

Ecce Homo!*
Ecce Deus!**

* Behold the man!   ** Behold your God!

Good Friday Intercessions

God of the crucified Jesus, we pray:

For the church:
that we may be courageous in carrying the cross,
compassionate in forgiving our enemies:
and willing to use our resources
in love for all for whom Jesus died.

For Australia:
that our Australian nation may be both just and generous:
and experience the grace that comes
from losing life and finding it.

For the suffering:
that sick, hungry, or suffering people
may know your love and receive your help
which they need physically, mentally, or spiritually:
In the fellowship of Christ's sufferings,
may they know there is a God who understands.

For our families and friends:
that, according to their individual needs,
your divine strength may be experienced in human weakness:
and that hopes that have been buried
may germinate and grow,
and be ready for a resurrection.

For each of us here:
that we may be lifted above anxieties, guilt,
bewilderment, pain, or fear,
and, by the mercy of the Jesus
who bore our sorrows and carried our shame,
find peace at the foot of the holy cross.
Blessed be your name,
God of the Crucified,
Friend of all the needy and forsaken.

Easter

God of the risen Christ and our God,
we rejoice in your resurrection power,
which is fully ours in Jesus Christ,
and we pray that you will keep us alert
to the sufferings, needs, or duties
that burden many people this Easter.

Keep us prayerfully aware of those
for whom this Easter is one of misery and loneliness:
  those who are separated from loved ones,
  immigrants who are lonely in a strange environment,
  alcoholics and other addicts
  for whom no day is ever a holiday,
  homeless young people,
  unwanted old people,
  and the inmates of our prisons:
*Living Lord, help them to know your love in the message of Easter,
and to rejoice in the gift of life in Christ.*

Keep us aware of those
for whom this Easter time is one of tragedy:
  especially the victims of road accidents,
  their family and friends,
  those who are seriously injured,
  those who are fighting for very life,
  and those who are weeping for the dead:
*Living Lord, help them to know your love in the message of Easter,
and to rejoice in the gift of life in Christ.*

Keep us aware, O God, also of those
who must work while most of
us are holidaying:
   policemen and prison warders,
   transport workers, and entertainers,
   ministers and priests,
   ambulance men and nurses,
   cooks and nightwatchmen,
   and all those who are busier than usual
   in catering for guests:
Living Lord, help them to know your love in the message of Easter,
and to rejoice in the gift of life in Christ.

God of Easter, keep each of us aware of our own needs,
and of the vast resources for our growth in faith, hope, and love,
which are available to us this day of resurrection:
through Jesus Christ our Lord.

Easter Mercies

Christ is risen:
He is risen indeed.
The King of glory is among us:
He entered the gates of our humanity.
Who is the King of glory?
The Lord of the stable and the cross,
He is the King of glory!

Who is this King of glory?
Jesus, the Word made flesh,
He is the King of glory!
He came to dwell among us,
and we saw his glory,
such glory as befits the Father's true Son,
full of grace and truth.
Christ is risen for us:
He is risen indeed! Hallelujah!

God of the risen Lord Jesus,
as we glory in your power
which raised up your Son,
give us more faith and hope;
help us to know
the availability of your power
in our weak lives.

When we despise and discourage ourselves,
Lord, have mercy:
Lord, have mercy.
When we despise and discourage others,
Christ, have mercy:
Christ, have mercy.
When we despise the grace of forgiveness,
maintaining the spirit of bondage,
Lord, have mercy:
Lord, have mercy.

(Silent meditation)

Hear the Gospel:
Christ is risen!
He is risen indeed!
Who dares condemn us?
Christ has died for us,
Christ is risen for us,
Christ intercedes for us.
What shall separate us
from the love of Christ?
Nothing,
Nothing today or tomorrow,
Nothing in life or death,
Shall separate us from God's love
in Christ Jesus our Lord.

The Right-hand Man

God of the humble and homeless,
    the poor and the persecuted,
thank you for exalting Christ Jesus
    and giving him a name
above all other names.

Today we rejoice
that he who was the meekest and weakest
    of all earth's children
is at your right hand.

Now we know
that the homeless Son of man
    is more truly at home
than anyone else on earth.

Today we rejoice
that he who was the poor teacher,
    who begged for a cup of water,
    and slept on the wild heath,
shows us our way to glory.

With gratitude we sing
    of the Man on a cross
who's now the exalted First-born
    of a new, everlasting race.

God of the defeated and the lonely,
    the despised and the hungry,
the misjudged and the imprisoned,
    the suffering and the dying,
we rejoice with great joy,
    praising his name,
and adoring your love!

City Pentecost

Through skyscraper canyons
    you come, Holy Spirit,
  down lanes and arcades
    you come:
  From the north, from the south,
  from within and without,
    like wind
    like wind
  the roar of Pure Wind,
  you come
  sweeping through
  to renew.

In houses of parliament
    you come, Holy Spirit,
  into lawmakers' chambers
    you come.
  From above, from below,
  from ally and foe,
    as truth
    as truth
  the roar of Pure Truth
  you come
  sweeping through
  to renew.

Through grand gothic arches
    you come, Holy Spirit,
  to choir and high altar
    you come.
  From the west, from the east,
  from the font and the feast,
    like fire
    like fire
  the roar of Pure Fire
  you come
  sweeping through
  to renew.

Pentecost Confession

If we have followed other spirits,
rather than the Spirit of Jesus,
Lord, have mercy:
Lord, have mercy.

If we have refused to give full rein
to the Spirit in our deeds and words,
Christ, have mercy:
Christ, have mercy.

So that we may be filled
with the loving fruits of the Spirit,
Lord, have mercy:
Lord, have mercy.

(Silent meditation)

The Spirit you have received is not a spirit of fear,
leading you back into slavery,
but the Spirit of adoption,
through which you call God
'Father, my very own Father'.

Spirit

Spirit of God, active in creation:
Spirit of love,
Spirit of Jesus, one with our Saviour:
Spirit of love,
Spirit of life, present in the Church:
Spirit of love.

We rejoice in your presence
around us and in us,
through the precious Gospel of Christ,
like wind on our faces
and breath in our lungs:
Presence of joy.

We rejoice in your power
to give new birth and new life,
like fire, warmth and radiance,
like life in dormant daffodils
bursting forth in spring:
Presence of hope.

We rejoice in your accepting us,
ceaselessly seeking us,
freely treasuring us,
with love older than mountains
or the distant stars,
new every morning:
Presence of grace.

Creator Spirit:
Spirit of love,
Life-giving Spirit:
Spirit of love,
Nurturing Spirit:
Spirit of love,
We bless you for your mercy,
love you and adore you.
Blessed be your name
of love for ever and ever.

Holy Spirit, Help Us

Holy Spirit, you make all things new;
renew us in will and deed
to work together with you.

That all people, who today are shivering
with an icy loneliness at the core of their being,
may let go, and let God fill them with his warmth:
Spirit, hear us; Spirit, help us.

That Christians may be more willing to trust the Spirit
to fill and renew their lives and relationships:
Spirit, hear us; Spirit, help us.

That disabled people, the sick, and the disadvantaged
may find the Spirit with them and in them,
giving new courage and serenity:
Spirit, hear us; Spirit, help us.

That bitter people, disillusioned people,
and the angry ones who cause war or terrorism,
may find an inner healing of the Spirit
that will lead to peace and reconciliation:
Spirit, hear us; Spirit, help us.

That those who cause or tolerate injustice and inhumanity
may be brought to repentance
and find the way of the compassionate Spirit:
Spirit, hear us; Spirit, help us.

Spirit of God,
Gift of Pentecost,
remake us in the likeness of Christ,
that we may live to your glory,
from here to eternity.

Trinity

When we lose faith in the goodness of creation,
and in the father-like love of our Creator:
Lord, have mercy.

When we lose faith in Jesus as the true reflection
of your suffering, death-conquering, redeeming love:
Christ, have mercy.
When we lose faith in your Spirit's presence among us,
working through your implanted Word:
Lord, have mercy.

Most loving God,
for the Word of mercy made flesh in Jesus Christ,
unmistakable and uncompromising in strong compassion:
we give you thanks.
For every word of love and forgiveness,
in individual people, in fellowship, and in prayer and worship:
we give you thanks.
For that insight or understanding within us,
that allows us to accept forgiveness
and to live with the joy of the freedom of God:
we give you thanks,
through Jesus Christ our Lord.

All Souls

Author of life abundant and eternal,
we thank you for the cloud of witnesses
  who make the mysterious heaven
  a home for our hearts.
Before you, we remember
  those faces we love
  and those spirits we treasure.

At radiant dawn
  and in the quiet of dusk:
we remember them.
Under summer skies
  with the farmlands shimmering:
we remember them.
Through winter's storms
  mid frost and snow:
we remember them.
At the return of spring
  with wattles clad in gold:
we remember them.
At birthdays and family celebrations,
  and in the festivals of the church:
we remember them.
When Christmas arrives
  with its carols and candles:
we remember them.
In the house of God
  as we sing and pray;
in the trumpets of the dawn
  on Easter Day;
in the Bread we break
and the Cup we take
  with eucharistic joy:
we remember them.

Our Paradox King

God of our Paradox King,
God of Bethlehem's son
and Nazareth's man,
Father of our Brother and Lord,
Friend of the poor:
Your name we adore,
Now and evermore.

King of the blind and the lame
and the leper with no name,
Jesus, Brother and Lord:
Your Spirit we love,
Your name we praise.

King of wild flowers and lilies,
ravens and sparrows,
Jesus, Brother and Lord:
Your Spirit we love,
Your name we praise.

King of lonely and outcast men,
and much-abased women,
Jesus, Brother and Lord:
Your Spirit we love,
Your name we praise.

King of all who are betrayed,
and those falsely tried,
Jesus, Brother and Lord:
Your Spirit we love,
Your name we praise.

King of the criminal dying,
and the forsaken crying,
Jesus, Brother and Lord:
Your Spirit we love,
your name we praise.

King of empty tombs and graves,
and limitless life,
Jesus, Brother and Lord:
Your Spirit we love,
Your name we praise.

God of the Paradox King,
love in the present,
love all transcendent,
Father of our Brother and Lord:
Your name we adore
now and evermore.

Part III
SMALL IS BEAUTIFUL
Collects on Various Themes

On Fieldlarks' Wings

As the fieldlark
rises at daybreak
to offer its praise
high above wheatfields,
trees, and farmhouses:

So may we,
in this hour of awakening,
let our gratitude ascend to you,
O Lord Most High.

On the Rays of the Morning

God of the inner light,
come to us
   on the golden rays of the morning,
   warming moods that are frosty,
   enlightening minds that are gloomy;
and, as the sun swings higher,
so may our lives rise to you
   in the active praise of this day's duties:
through Jesus, our risen Light.

Trusting New Life

Spirit of new life,
grant unto us this day
   the grace to recognize new life
   breaking through
   in unlikely events;
and, in so recognizing it,
   to be ready to trust it
   and delight in it:
through Jesus Christ our Lord.

Twentieth-Century Saints

Most loving God,
hope and joy of all who are
pure,
humble,
poor,
hungry,
merciful,
and ready to suffer for righteousness' sake:
Keep us faithful in the love of Jesus,
that we may be his twentieth-century saints and disciples:
In his loving, saving name.

As Eagle and Dolphin

O God, you are my God:
early will I seek you,
my soul thirsts for you,
my flesh longs for you.
As the eagle belongs to the air,
and the dolphin belongs to the sea,
so we belong to you,
O God, my God.

Daybreak

Most loving God,
we who worship in the early hours of this day
pray for the grace
to accept all duties and pleasures
as a gift from you,
and by the help of your Spirit
to allow all things
to work together for good:
through Jesus Christ our Lord.

Touch and Heal Us

Most loving God,
   in whom we live and move
   and have our being,
give us new awareness of your presence.

Touch our minds,
   that we may know you
   in the word of Scripture
   and in the living Word, Jesus Christ.
Touch our ears,
   that we may hear you in music and song.
Touch our eyes,
   that we may remember you
   in the signs of cross and candlelight.
Touch our hearts,
   that we may love you
   with a love that sweeps through us
   like a great tide.

Living, loving Spirit of God,
touch us with the spirit
of love, joy, and praise.

Like a Plover

God, tender and strong,
  as the plover defends her young
  against their enemies,
so defend me
  against those anxieties and nameless fears
  which are my enemies.
Save me in the hour of trial,
  and deliver me from evil.
Under your wings
  let me shelter
until faith and courage return:
for your love's sake.

For Lightweights

Most wonderful God,
great strength is yours
to exert at every moment:
  look gently upon our frailty.
And, although we weigh no more
than a grain of sand or a drop of dew,
  fill us with your Spirit
that we may become weighty
in matters of grace, mercy, and peace:
through Jesus Christ our Lord.

Divine Generosity

Generous God,
Your open-handedness goes far beyond what we deserve,
and higher than our noblest aspirations.

We do not ask for more blessings,
but for the ability
to recognize, enjoy, and extol
the ones that are ours for the taking:
through Jesus Christ our Lord.

Morning

Creating God,
   as the curtain of night is drawn back,
   and the golden robes of the day
   arrive over sea and mountain,
expel from our minds all sour thoughts,
that we may greet this new day as a gift
   fresh from the hands of creation,
   and filled with hope, and bright with gladness,
and glorify the One who makes all things new:
through Jesus Christ our Lord.

The Word and the Babble

Loving God,
give us a lively and sensitive mind
that we may hear your Word
above the babble of human words;
and, so hearing,
may follow every suggestion
you make to us this day:
through Jesus Christ our Lord.

Unspeakable Joys

Loving God,
you have knit together your people
in one communion and community
within the mystical body of Jesus Christ.
Give us grace
so to follow your saints
in all faithful living,
that we may participate in the unspeakable joys
which you have prepared for all who love you:
through Jesus Christ our Lord.

Needed Gifts

Give us, O God,
diligence to seek you,
wisdom to recognize you,
purity of heart to know you,
and a faith
that may love and embrace you:
through Jesus Christ our Lord.

Listen to Our Brother

Almighty God,
   you are the source of all life.
Help us, your children, to listen
to our Elder Brother,
Jesus the Christ,
   that in him we may discover
   the fullness of life,
   and be delivered from all false goals
   and all crippling fears:
through Jesus Christ our Lord.

Reedwarbler

Lord of peace,
at this evening hour
under the open skies,
create within my soul
a vesper as pure
as this melody
which rises near the riverbank
from the throat
of your little reedwarbler.

God of the Evening

Now that dusk is near —
   with parrots in the gum trees
   lessening their chatter,
   with the distant roar of cars
   fading to a mere murmur —
may I hear
the 'voice of the One
who walks in the garden
in the cool of the evening',
   and, in hearing that voice,
find a little of the Eden-peace
which some day will be perfected.
This I pray
in the name of him
who was once mistaken for a gardener.

Joy on Grey Days

Joyful Spirit, Holy God,
   on grey days which dawn
   but slowly and sullenly,
still give us the grace
   to sing with the magpie,
   and laugh with the kookaburra:
through Jesus Christ our Lord.

Bonuses

God of grace and God of glory,
you have invited us to share
the bonuses and burdens of your kingdom
with Jesus
our Elder Brother;
grant that we may continue to accept your offer,
and bring forth deeds of grace
after the example of our Christ:
in whose name we pray.

When Honour Departs

O Lord, our Lord,
   as times arrive when it is appropriate for us
   to relinquish tasks and positions
   which have brought pleasure and honour to us,
help us to do so
with the dignity and beauty
of the poplar trees in autumn,
   so that, in both gaining and losing,
   we may live to your glory:
through Jesus Christ our Lord.

A Quiet Spirit

Teach us, good Lord,
to pray as we should,
so that we, who so often babble
like the heathen,
may be released from our much asking,
and brought to rest our lives
in the hands of the Father
who knows our needs before we ask him.

Victorious

O God,
You raised up your true Son
   to crush evil and give us abundant life.
Grant that, filled with this Gospel,
   we may seek the company of Christ Jesus,
so that in his nurturing friendship
   we also may become victors over all evil,
and begin now the promised life of the ages.
This we pray in his name.

New Year's Eve: Endings and Beginnings

God of things old and things new,
   of precious memories and exciting hopes,
help us to complete this old phase of our life,
and to begin the new
   in the peace, joy, and courage to be,
   which is your personal gift
   to all who will receive it:
through Christ Jesus,
the hope of yesterday,
today, and for ever.

This New Day

Most loving God,
you have given us this new day
in which to serve you
and to delight in you.

By your Spirit help us to do so,
not as slaves,
but as your precious children,
called to be the sisters and brothers
of our Lord Jesus Christ,
in whose name we gather this morning.

Incarnation

Almighty God,
you have wonderfully created us,
and even more wonderfully saved us
through the holy incarnation.
Grant, we pray,
that, as Jesus completely shared our nature,
we may increasingly share his spirit
and live to your glory,
and thus inherit the life abundant
which you have prepared for us
in and through Jesus Christ our Lord.

Hearing the Angels' Song

Most wonderful God,
   whose glory angels sang
   when Christ was born,
help us who hear the good news
truly to know it,
and, in knowing it, to believe,
and, in believing, to obey —
   that we may rejoice in your peace,
   and live to love one another
   even as you have loved us:
through Jesus Christ our Lord.

Faith

Living God,
   faith is your gift to us.
We thank you for the faith we have,
and pray you to enlarge it,
   so that, by faith,
   our hope in you will be more radiant,
   and our love purer, stronger,
   and more courageous:
through Jesus Christ our Lord.

Christ the King

God,
we thank you for Jesus,
  our Prince of peace
  and our King of love.
Blessed by his love,
and freed by his forgiveness,
may we follow that royal way
which exalts
  forgiveness,
  mercy,
  truth,
  generosity,
  courage,
  compassion,
  and faithfulness.
This we ask for his name's sake.

Advent

O God,
you make us glad each year
when we remember
the birth of Jesus.

Grant that we may
joyfully receive him as Redeemer,
serve him as Lord,
and love him as Brother and Friend,
now and for ever.

Partners in Love

God of new creation,
we thank you that ultimately
   there is only one energy
that links all together:
   the vigour of your love.
Grant that this day
   we may be partners with you in love,
and so bring out into the open
   the glory which so often lies hidden:
through Jesus Christ our Lord.

Good Shepherd

Most loving God,
in Jesus, who gave his life for the sheep,
you have opened up to us
the way of limitless life.

Help us to know Jesus our Good Shepherd,
   that we may be able to recognize his voice
   among the many voices that call to us;
and, knowing his voice,
may we have the courage
   to follow wherever he leads us,
that our lives may be opened
to the limitless life
which you offer to all your children.

This we pray,
in the name of our Good Shepherd,
Christ Jesus our Brother and Lord.

Part IV

GO IN PEACE
Confession and Forgiveness

Shame and Glory

Most loving God,
we admit to you and to each other
that we are beings in whom shame and glory
are strangely mixed.
We are creatures of wisdom and folly,
    trust and anxiety, success and failure,
    truth and deceit, love and apathy.
We need you, yet we evade you —
    to believe, yet we doubt,
    to praise, yet dishonour,
    to love, yet resent.
God of the new creation and our God,
we wish to be made whole
    in thought, word, and deed.
We seek of you today the gifts of Jesus:
    forgiveness, renewal,
    self-acceptance, self-understanding,
and the courage to be
the sisters and brothers of Christ.

To Be More Loving

God of grace, God of glory,
  we turn to you
  for the word of forgiveness and new life.

When we criticize others
for the same weakness that lies hidden in us:
Save us, good Lord.
When we take a legalistic attitude
rather than the difficult stance of love:
Save us, good Lord.
So that we may live the law of love
in all its discipline and freedom:
Save us, good Lord.

Loving God,
we thank you that through Christ Jesus
you have saved us,
you are saving us,
and you will save us.

Losing Faith

All knowledge is yours, O God,
   and you know us better
   than we know ourselves.

If we lose faith in ourselves as your children:
Forgive and restore us.
If we lose faith in your pervasive goodness and mercy:
Forgive and restore us.
If we lose faith in the Word that, where sin abounds,
grace much more abounds:
Forgive and restore us.

All knowledge is yours, O God,
   and all love comes from you.
In your own wise way and at your time,
transform us into the people
   you would have us be:
through Jesus Christ our Lord.

When We Fail to Love

Jesus said: Everything in the law and the prophets hangs on two things:
You shall love the Lord your God,
with all your heart and soul,
and mind and strength;
and you shall love your neighbour as yourself.

I confess to you, most loving God,
and to you, my Christian family,
that, although I honour Jesus Christ,
I fall far short of his example.

I am a disciple of little faith.
My loyalty wavers, my vision is limited;
my prayers are selfish, and my sacrifice is rare.
I confess that my love for God and my neighbour too readily grows cold.

But, despite our sin, we know
our God is merciful.
I pray for the forgiveness that renovated Peter,
the compassion that healed Magdalene,
the grace that accepted Thomas,
and the love that wiped away the tears of Mary.

Who shall rescue us from this body of defeat and death?
God alone, through Jesus Christ our Lord!

Lord, we hear your voice:
Child, your sins are forgiven you;
go in peace.
Thank you, God of faithfulness,
love, and new life.

Failure to Love

Living God,
you raised Jesus from death
to be the power of saving love
in our midst.

We confess our failure
    to entertain and trust his love.
We have not loved you, God,
    with his fervent love.
We have not loved others
    with his class of love.
We have not even loved ourselves enough
    to cherish and nurture our own lives
    in the ways of Christ Jesus.

As a result, our characters are stunted,
    our lives mis-shapen,
    and too often, fruitless.

Have mercy on us, we pray.
Break down all the barriers
    which we erect against your love.
Enter the dark or dusty places of our being,
    purifying and enlightening us.

Restore to us
    the joy of your salvation,
and renew a right spirit within us.
May Jesus Christ grow larger
    in all our activities:
In his gracious saving name.

Faith and Works

If we have become obsessed with the needs of our own soul,
and neglected the deeds of faith:
Forgive us, merciful Lord.

If we have become so preoccupied with good works
that we have neglected your nurturing grace for our spirit:
Forgive us, merciful Lord.

That we may be possessed
by the lovely, balanced spirit of Jesus our Christ,
bringing health to our prayers and deeds:
Take us over, merciful Lord.

We thank you for this moment of honesty and insight,
and for the assurance of your saving grace.
*Blessed be your lovely and loving name
for ever.*

To Know Ourselves

Most merciful God,
help us this morning to trust your grace —
  more than misers do richness,
  or politicians power.

That we may know ourselves through and through,
yet not be afraid:
Lord, have mercy.

That we may frankly face
our foolishness and our shortcomings,
yet not be despairing:
Christ, have mercy.

That we may be aware of
our gifts, virtues, and strengths,
and not hide them under a fake humility:
Lord, have mercy.

Where sin abounds,
grace much more abounds:
The law came through Moses,
but grace and truth
through Jesus Christ our Lord.

Hurry and Worry

God of eternity, creator of time,
giver of life and love,
rescue us from those pressures
which throw us off balance.

If today we have been in too much of a hurry
to realize that it is good to be alive:
Lord, have mercy.

If we live too close to the news headlines,
and not close enough to the eternal verities:
Christ, have mercy.

If we become so worried
that we forget that your grace is sufficient for us:
Lord, have mercy.

Timeless God, steadfast in love,
generous and patient with all your creatures:
*let the peace of our Lord, Jesus the Christ,
garrison our lives this day.*

Lost in the Traffic

Because we become confused in the traffic of life,
and easily lose our way:
Lord, have mercy.
Because we often seem unable to transform wrong turnings
into opportunities for grace and growth:
Lord, have mercy.
So that we may see more clearly, act more creatively,
and move forward with the courage of our convictions:
Lord, have mercy.

Most merciful God,
who alone can help us find our true direction,
deliver us from confusion,
   defend us in temptation,
strengthen us in weakness,
   and keep us on the road
which Jesus has taken.

Double Standards

Because we get angry about trivial matters,
but remain apathetic in the midst of grave injustices:
Lord, have mercy.
Because we take a rigid stance when criticizing others,
yet plead special consideration and understanding for ourselves:
Christ, have mercy.
Because we readily legalize the old commandments,
and sentimentalize the new commandment:
Lord, have mercy.

God of Jesus, help us
to turn from our double standards,
to accept your acceptance,
to discard our guilt and anxiety,
to make amends where it is possible,
and then to get on with business of living in the Spirit.
In the name of our Lord, we pray.

Judge Not

Because we indulge in the destructive sin
of dividing people into rigid categories of good and bad:
Lord, have mercy.
Because we attempt to bolster our own ego
by playing at being judge:
Christ, have mercy.
So that we may encourage and assist
people who despise themselves to stand up tall:
Lord, have mercy.
God with us,
Spirit of truth,
you are present everywhere,
    filling all things;
treasury of love,
    the reservoir of life,
please dwell in us.
Remove all ugliness,
and foster health in every part:
through Jesus Christ our Lord.

For Recovery of Joy and Liberty

Because we too readily become discouraged
and half-hearted about our discipleship:
Lord, have mercy.
Because we allow our values and attitudes
to be distorted by the pressures of society:
Christ, have mercy.
So that we may recover our joy in the Gospel
and our liberty in loving service:
Lord, have mercy.

Lord, we pray that your grace
may always precede and follow us,
and enable us continually to give ourselves
to the good works of your new world:
through Jesus Christ our Lord.

Bring Us to Our Senses

Loving God,
because we carry burdens on our own shoulders
that we could have shared with you:
Lord, have mercy, and bring us to our senses.
Because we have listened to many conflicting voices in society,
and failed to take time to listen to your still, small voice:
Christ, have mercy, and bring us to our senses.
So that we may be freed from guilt and needless anxiety,
and experience the peace of forgiveness and renewal:
Lord, have mercy, and bring us to our senses.

All-pervasive God,
   in whom we live and move and have our being,
so guide us in the ways of mercy and truth,
and rule us by your Spirit,
   that, in all the cares and occupations of life,
we may keep cool heads and loving hearts,
   as we walk the way
of our Lord and Saviour, Jesus Christ.

Part V

GOOD TO BE ALIVE
Thanksgiving and Praise

Full of Grace and Truth

In the thick of a crowd —
  some hearing,
  some fearing,
weary woman forces through,
  touches his hem,
  is whole again:
Glory to the Son,
full of grace and truth.

When the sun is setting —
  the crowds now gone,
  he, now alone,
climbs the near mountain,
  finds the grace
  of a solitary place:
Glory to the Son,
full of grace and truth.

At the dawn of a day —
  he is beholding
  wild heath unfolding,
Solomon far outstripped,
  bellbirds ringing,
  magpies singing:
Glory to the Son,
full of grace and truth.

In a proud man's house —
  tired, reclining,
  harlot arriving,
washes his feet with tears,
  her shame released,
  goes in his peace:
Glory to the Son,
full of grace and truth.

In an olive grove lonely —
    vigil keeping,
    courage seeking
to drink the bitter cup:
    sweat-blood falling,
    agony appalling:
Glory to the Son,
full of grace and truth.

Nailed to rough wood —
    life-blood spending,
    heavens unbending
at the cry of him forsaken,
    gasping, crying,
    alone in dying:
Glory to the Son,
full of grace and truth.

Beside waters at dawn —
    fishermen trawling,
    Stranger calling:
'Throw wide the nets',
    breakfast prepared
    served by the Lord:
Glory to the Son,
full of grace and truth.
Glory, glory,
Glory to the Son,
Firstborn of the children of God.

Gloria In Excelsis

Yours is the glory:
　　Light in the word
　　Word in the silence
　　Warmth in the cold
　　Life in the cell
　　Love at the threshold.
Yours is the glory
Beginning and end.

Yours is the glory:
　　Light over Eden
　　Dust standing tall
　　Praying and crying
　　Loving and losing
　　Laughing and sighing.
Yours is the glory
Beginning and end.

Yours is the glory:
　　Light over Bethlehem
　　Laughter in Nazareth
　　Sunshine through Galilee
　　Gloom in Gethsemane
　　Cloud over Calvary.
Yours is the glory
Beginning and end.

Yours is the glory:
　　Light from a tomb
　　Love new arising
　　Greeting and mending
　　Renewing indwelling
　　Trusting and sending.
Yours is the glory
Beginning and end.

Yours is the glory:
 Light in community
 People enlivened
 Liberated and caring
 Body of Jesus
 Impudent and daring.
Yours is the glory
Beginning and end.

The Name: Jesus

For the name of Jesus, Saviour, and the Word made flesh:
Blessed be the Lord God.

That we are forgiven:
Blessed be the Lord God.

That we are rescued and accepted by love divine:
Blessed be the Lord God.

That his name is Emmanuel, God with us:
Blessed be the Lord God.

That we are adopted into the family of God,
and are indeed sisters and brothers of Jesus:
Blessed be the Lord God.

That nothing in life or death,
earth or heaven, past, present or future,
can separate us from the love of Christ:
Blessed be the Lord God,
For he has visited and redeemed his people!

Endless Love

We thank you, God,
through our Lord Jesus Christ,
for the assurance of forgiveness
and the promise of renewal.
Your everlasting name
is mercy and love.
At morning, noon, and night,
You are mercy and love.

You are compassion;
Your love never ends.
You are our hope;
Your love never ends.
You are our inspiration;
Your love never ends.
You are true liberty;
Your love never ends.
You are joy and peace;
Your love never ends.

At morning, noon, and night,
you are mercy and love.
Holy is your name
above all names;
and, by your grace,
holy is our gratitude:
through Jesus Christ,
our Saviour and our Brother.

Focus

God of light,
    Father of the True-man,
    when we commune with him
    we find the clear focus
    for every scattered ray of light
    that has warmed our day
    or cheered our night.

Encountering him,
    all fond theories
    and all other options —
    no matter how brave
    or seductive to reason —
    become mere chatter
    and games of evasion.

Through him alone
    you offer that sheer grace
    which can create much
    out of very little —
    or out of nothing,
    in our darkest hours,
    make everything.

Your relentless Christ
    leaves nothing unchallenged,
    nothing unused;
    every seed of faith
    is nurtured and warmed,
    while every vagrant aim
    becomes transformed.

Though he lives large,
    Man ahead of man,
    he never engulfs us
    nor deserts us in the ruck;
    the irreversible cross
    and discarded tomb
    allow no loss.

Baptized by the Morning

Risen Lord Jesus,
as the rising sun
baptizes trees and shrubs
in rippling light,
let me be baptized
by your resurrection light.

May I
trust in you above all else,
hope in you above all other goals,
seek you in all things,
find you in every situation,
meet you among all people,
know you over everything —

And love you with adoration
beyond
beyond
beyond all telling.

Great Thanksgiving

Lift up your hearts:
We lift them to the Lord.

Let us give thanks to the Lord our God:
It is right to give him thanks and praise.

For this lovely planet, earth;
for its beauty and fertility;
for the human family with its many races and faces;
and for Your utter faithfulness to us
in spite of our rebellion and sin:
In the name of the Father, most generous Creator, we thank you.

For the deeds and words of the prophets and saints;
for the Word made flesh in Jesus our Brother
who lived among us, suffered and died for us,
and rose with abundant life:
In the name of the Son, most gracious Redeemer, we thank you.

For your renewing presence, creating the Church
and inspiring deeds of justice and love:
In the name of the Spirit, most Holy Comforter, we thank you.

With angels and archangels,
and with all the company of heaven,
we proclaim your great and glorious name,
for ever praising you and singing:
Holy, holy, holy Lord, God of power and might,
heaven and earth are full of your glory.
Hosanna in the highest.

Blessed is he who comes in the name of the Lord.
Hosanna in the highest.

Thanksgiving for Light

Most wonderful God, we thank you for the gift of light:
For its power to cheer us, enliven us, encourage and guard us.
For the merry old sun, rising over our hills and calling us to a new day:
For moonlight and starlight, stirring a sense of wonder
and serenity within us.

For street light, car light, traffic light, protecting
and guiding us:
For the beauty of city lights viewed from the hills.
For the beauty of affection lighting the faces of those
who love us:
For the light of human compassion in hospitals, nursing
homes, and counselling agencies.

For the supreme light of divine love
in the face of the Man of Nazareth:
For the radiance of Christ's goodness, grace, and
self-sacrifice.
For his light in his church, exposing, challenging, and
showing us the way to new creation:
For his radiance in our individual lives, uncovering,
rebuking, forgiving, renewing, and guiding us.
Most wonderful God, we praise you
for the Light of the world:
Most merciful God, we praise you
for the Sun that is never eclipsed!
God of God, Light of Light,
Glory be to you now and for ever.

Evening Prayer

The busy day now takes its rest,
as mother evening enfolds us in embrace.
The distant stars and galaxies signal
messages about a Creator so vast
that our minds stagger
and our hearts are filled
with loving awe.

O Lord, our Lord,
glorious is your name in all the universe.
What are earth's children
that you notice us?
And what is the mystery of divine grace
that you love us?
You give us faith to trust you,
even though we cannot see you.
You touch our minds with fingers of light,
and our hearts with forgiveness and peace.

As the evening moves on,
we go to rest
able to sleep the sleep of children
who know that, in life or death,
we are surrounded by love eternal.

O Lord, our Lord, glorious is your name
on earth and in the heavens!

Good to be Alive!

God, our Father in Christ,
it is good to be alive,
to share life with each other
in your wonderful creation:
We are most grateful,
and we thank you, Lord.

You have given us the opportunity
to see the spring flowers,
to watch trees in the wind,
to inhale the fragrance of the season,
and to feel the warmth of the air:
We are most grateful,
and we thank you, Lord.

God, it is good to rest in the evening,
and rise in the morning,
to walk upon this good earth,
to hear your whisper in many places,
and to sing your praise with many friends:
We are most grateful,
and we thank you, Lord.

Lord, like a generous friend
you share the whole world with us,
and you fill our cup to overflowing
with the wine of gladness:
We are most grateful,
and we thank you, Lord.

We want to sing, dance, and pray,
in gratitude for every good thing in your creation!
Especially we want to embrace and express your Spirit;
the Spirit that filled our Lord Jesus to overflowing,
the Spirit of mercy, forgiveness, courage, and new life;
the Spirit of love, and laughter, and peace:
We are most grateful,
and we thank you, Lord.

For your presence with us, around us, beneath us,
within us, behind us, and in front of us:
we, your children, are most grateful,
and we thank you, through Jesus Christ our Lord.

For Faith

Most wonderful God,
we thank you for the faith we have;
help us to trust you more.

We thank you
for all that keeps us believing
   that our lives have meaning,
that our coming and going
   are noticed by our Heavenly Father,
that disappointment, sickness, fear, or death
   does not cut us off from you,
that always there shines
   the light of Jesus Christ
to sparkle in our happiness
   or lighten our darkest hours.

We thank you
for the meaning given to us
   by those who love and cherish us;
for the purpose injected into our lives
   by wise friends and counsellors;
for the fellowship of the Church
and the wisdom of the Holy Bible;
   for the love which your Spirit spreads in our hearts.

We thank you
   for our faith in grace and mercy,
   for the call to repentance,
   the forgiveness of sins,
   the constant miracle of a new start —
all made possible
through what you have done,
and are still doing,
through Jesus, our Brother and Lord.

Most wonderful God,
    may an awareness of your divine love
soak through our every artery and vein,
    every nerve, tissue, and muscle,
through every cell of our brain
    and into the mysterious depths of our soul,
till we respond to you
    with every fibre of our being,
and worship you as you deserve:
through Jesus Christ our Lord.

Good Morning

The dew is a thousand eyes
shining across the parkland.

The silk sculpture of the spider
glistens between rails on the fence.

May everybody outdoors this morning,
from the grandmother collecting milk
to the pyjama-clad child on her trike,
    know that life is good,
    the world is beautiful,
    and that You, Creating Spirit,
    are the Highest Good
    and the Most Beautiful!

Good morning,
O Lord,
Good morning!
Glorious is your name
in all the earth.

Special People

We thank you, O God,
for those people who are channels of your love in our lives:
For those who gave us birth,
and, in the weakness of our infancy,
sheltered, nurtured, and treasured us.

For those who taught us to walk,
to talk and to explore tastes, smells, sounds,
and to experience the warmth
of belonging and embracing.

For those who overlooked our faults
and affirmed our strengths,
and the friends young and old
who share our tears and laughter.

We thank you, Lord,
for the people of strong faith
who stretch our minds and enlarge our capacity
to explore and understand your ways.

For those at every stage of our journey
who teach us trust by trusting us,
who enable us to love others
through the experience of being loved.

We thank you for those very sincere people
who have demonstrated the joys and disciplines
of the kingdom of God,
and especially people who taught us to love you,
rather than to be afraid of you.

God of love, God of Jesus,
for these healing experiences of growth and loving,
and for the knowledge that the best is yet to come,
we praise your holy name:
through Jesus Christ our Lord.

A Child's Gratitude

Dear God,
thank you for letting us live
in your wonderful world!

Thank you for
kookaburra and kangaroo,
koala, emu, parrot, possum,
pelican, brolga, and willy wagtail.

Thank you for our pets:
dogs which run to meet us,
the purring of cats,
the singing of canaries,
and the chatter of budgies.

Thank you, God,
for playmates and schoolmates,
penfriends and church friends,
for the kindness of grandparents,
and the care of mother and father.

Thank you, God,
for all good and beautiful things —
and most of all for Jesus
who brings us your great love for us.

Springtime

Most wonderful God,
all your works praise you,
speaking your glory and singing of your grace:
We thank you, Lord.

For the changing mood of nature,
with the promise of a springtime soon to come
and its signs around us:
We thank you, Lord.

For the wattle putting on its golden robe,
the almond blossom purer than snow,
for the white and pink heath in our hills,
for the growing cheerfulness of birds,
singing their songs at dusk and dawn:
We thank you, Lord.

For the renewing pleasures of human love and friendship,
for friends returning from holidays,
for loved ones close to us,
for letters and cards telling of births,
engagements, weddings, and travel:
We thank you, Lord.

For the deep-down springtimes of heart, mind, and soul,
spiritual insights and new joys,
music, art, prayers, books — and the Holy Bible,
and the uplift of a congregation
singing the new songs of faith:
We thank you, Lord.

For the call to new life of Jesus Christ,
the word that gives challenge and encouragement,
the life that awakens the hopes of the world:
We thank you, Lord.

For the ministry of the Holy Spirit right now,
for the divine love at hand
to forgive and renew like living water,
washing away all that is sordid, guilty, and unlovely,
and allowing the new growth of faith and hope to take over:
We give you thanks and praise,
through Jesus Christ our Lord.

For All His Mercies

For the forgiveness of sins
and the renewal of our self-respect —
give thanks to the Lord,
for he is good:
His mercy endures for ever.

For the ministries of the church
in pastoral care, music,
fellowship, service,
education, prayer,
and the challenge of the living Word —
give thanks to the Lord,
for he is good:
His mercy endures for ever.

For daily life,
with its sunshine and rain,
toil and rest,
food and drink,
love and friendship,
tears and laughter —
give thanks to the Lord,
for he is good:
His mercy endures for ever.

For people who love us enough
to put up with us when we are irritable,
thoughtless, selfish, or unkind —
give thanks to the Lord,
for he is good:
His mercy endures for ever.

For the generous bonus
of knowing the love of God
through Jesus Christ,
that in him we live and move
and have our being —
give thanks to the Lord,
for he is good:
His mercy endures for ever.

Part VI

LOVE YOUR NEIGHBOUR
Sharing the Concerns of the Lord

Inasmuch

Lord most merciful,
you meet us in unexpected places and people.
Help us to be alert to meet you,
That you may heal our wounds,
and make us ready to serve you
in the needs of our neighbours.

Where you are hungry and homeless,
help us to be your loving people,
giving food and shelter:
Help us to be alert to meet you.

Where you are imprisoned or oppressed,
help us to be your liberated people,
giving comfort and help:
Help us to be alert to meet you.

Where you are anxious and despairing,
help us to be your concerned people,
sharing hope and encouragement:
Help us to be alert to meet you.

Where you are sick and dying,
help us to be your consoling people,
standing at your side with comfort and a steadying hand:
Help us to be alert to meet you.

Where you are the victim of violence and warfare,
help us to be your peace-filled people,
active in peacemaking and rich in love.
Help us to be alert to meet you.

And to you alone,
ever-living and ever-loving God,
be the praise of our lips
and the service of our lives,
now and for ever.

Where People Live

Where people live with a bitterness of spirit
which poisons and distresses those around them:
Your kingdom come.

Where people live greedily, without gratitude or grace,
keeping a ruthless eye on the possessions of others:
Your kingdom come.

Where folk resort to violence, rape, terrorism, and warfare,
spreading suffering and accelerating hatreds:
Your kingdom come.

Where people suffer disease, handicap, or savage injustice,
without any faith to support them:
Lord, your kingdom come.

Where communities of mixed races
ache with ugly fears and hatreds,
and the grief which follows repression or violence:
Lord, your kingdom come.

For all who sit with the dying,
make funeral arrangements,
or spend tonight sleepless and grieving,
we pray for the gift of divine comfort.

Lord, your kingdom come,
Your will be done
on earth as it is in heaven,
through Jesus Christ our Lord.

Transforming Misfortunes

Most loving God,
in this cynical world help your people
to prove the hopefulness of existence
by turning negative situations into positive ones:
When we are weak, then we are strong.

Help folk to transform
disappointments into new courage,
or pain into greater caring and sharing:
When we are weak, then we are strong.

Help people to use sickness
for increased sensitivity toward all who suffer or grieve,
and to make us treasure our neighbours all the more:
When we are weak, then we are strong.

Help us all to use reproach for honest self-assessment,
and abuse for better understanding of others who are abused:
When we are weak, then we are strong.

Help the lost to use their dismay
to spur them into finding themselves and their true destiny:
When we are weak, then we are strong.

Help each of us here
to find your word though prayers seem unanswered,
and to hear your call in difficult opportunities:
*We can do all things through Christ
who strengthens us.*

Our City

God of Jesus,
we pray this morning for our fair city of ..., your gift to us.

We think of its character
noble in history,
proud of its founders,
but often blind
to the source of their inspiration.

Lord, we are proud of its cultures, but troubled about its soul,
proud of its festivals, but troubled about its unemployment.
For some it is the scene of their success-story;
for others it is the place of poverty,
injustice, neglect, and despair.

Merciful God,
help this our city, and your city.

We pray for the city council,
the police, the magistrates,
social workers, town planners,
schools, hospitals, transport authorities,
the directors of big business-houses,
and all the community organizations
who work for the health of our city.

King of the 'City Splendid',
help us to make our city
closer to the city
you would have it be,
through your life-changing love in Jesus Christ our Lord.

Strengthen Our Resolve

Let us pray for others.

For the church:
that it may be released from all adultery
with materialistic culture and power;
God, hear our prayer:
Lord, strengthen our resolve.

For our Australian nation:
that political idols may be broken,
and covetousness lose its power over us;
God, hear our prayer:
Lord, strengthen our resolve.

For the nations of the world:
that false witness by the manipulators may be exposed,
stealing from the weak by the strong be outlawed,
and killing by suppression, starvation, terrorism, or war
be banished for ever;
God, hear our prayer:
Lord, strengthen our resolve.
In the name of Jesus Christ, we pray.

Our Indigenous People

God of our ancient people,
Lord of all tribes,
show those of us who are
more-recent arrivals
in this great south land
how best we can allow Aborigines
to recover their dignity,
and to make their rich contribution
to the well-being of our growing nation.

Thank you for those in government,
and in the church community,
who are really listening
and responding with true wisdom
to their needs and cries.
Thank you for some land rights restored,
for much progress among tribal groups,
for emerging aboriginal poets,
priests, ministers, and managers.

We pray with anguished soul
for the descendants of tribes
disinherited long ago,
for those broken spirits
who gather without aim or hope,
in parks and lanes of cities and towns.
Lord, we feel incapable of discovering
how we can help —
except perhaps to admit to them
that we are burdened to belong
to the race that helped corrupt them.

Lord, hear our cry;
Many of us long to undo
the many wrongs,
as far as that is possible.
But how do we start, Lord?
Where do we start?
Lord, hear our cry!

Planting True Vines

Make our lives, good Lord,
through Jesus our true Vine,
living branches of faith, hope, and love
so that the existence of others may be enriched
and our own lives grow mature with the fruits of Jesus Christ.

For our brothers and sisters
in all their diverse needs,
we pray.

Where people have forgotten how to laugh,
touch them with your joy.
Where they have lost the art of mercy,
graft compassion and forgiveness within them.
Where they neglect to share bread, medicine, trust and friendship,
stir new growth of love within them.

Lord,
our true Vine,
abide in us
that we may abide in you.

Let your presence support the weak,
encourage the sick,
comfort the dying,
guide the confused,
heal the broken-hearted,
soften the hard heart,
and sweeten the bitter spirit.

Let the harvest of our prayers,
be in your time
and in your way, most loving Lord.

For Church and World

Prayer for a Civic Service

In faith, hope and love, let us seek God's blessing on his world and his Church.

Let us pray:
For the church of Jesus Christ in all its branches, in all the world, for the churches of this nation, this State and this city, enabling the community of faith to embody the words and deeds of Christ Jesus:
Lord, hear our humble prayer.
For the head of our Commonwealth, your servant Elizabeth our Queen, and for all governors, governments, councils, and courts under her, that we may be led in the ways of those who thirst for righteousness and hunger for peace:
Lord, hear our humble prayer.
For all nations, both our allies and our enemies, that there may be an end to all injustice, poverty, persecution, and especially for a just reconciliation between warring factions;
Lord, hear our humble prayer.
For those among our family or neighbours, colleagues or friends, who are at present living through difficult days of sickness, sorrow, injury, injustice, anxiety or bitterness, that they may discover the loving resources of the Holy Spirit:
Lord, hear our humble prayer.
For each person in this congregation today, with personal worry, heartache, pain or distress, and especially for anyone who feels that they are at the end of their tether, that these be given recovery of courage and peace of mind:
Lord, hear our humble prayer.
Most loving God, source of all grace, light, and peace, restore to all people the joy and health of your salvation, through Jesus Christ our Lord.

For Those who Hunger

God of Jesus, God of us all,
Only true and everlasting friend,
inspire us to pray and act with the compassion of Jesus Christ.

God, at this moment there are people who hunger for food,
   for a crust of bread, a piece of fish,
   or even the scraps in our garbage bins.
Please feed them:
Lord, hear our prayer, and make us your answer to prayer.

There are some people who hunger for liberty,
   to go as they please,
   to stay on at home or visit friends,
   to worship without hindrance,
   to vote for whom they please,
   to see the end of police, compounds, and prisons,
   to be reunited with those they love dearly.
Please give them liberty:
Lord, hear our prayer, and make us your answer to prayer.

And there are some who hunger to be useful,
   to share what wisdom they have learnt from life,
   to listen to a neighbour's worries,
   to work beside a weary friend,
   to be of use to their family, country or church —
   to be of use to you;
   but bad health,
   or shyness and timidity,
   or unsightly physical deformity,
   or the frailty of old age,
   or sorrow over old sins,
   holds them back and makes them useless.
Please show them how they can still be useful:
Lord, hear our prayer, and make us your answer to prayer.

Loving Father, there are some who hunger for your grace,
   who look for faith,
   who search for your meaning and your name,
   who look for someone whom they can trust,
   and hunger for something worth worshipping.
Please satisfy their hunger with the bread of life:
Lord, hear our prayer, and make us your answer to prayer.

And to you, dear Lord,
Father and Provider,
Christ and Saviour,
Holy Spirit and Friend,
be honour and glory,
worship and praise,
from now to eternity.

The Way of Truth

A Prayer of Young People

Spirit of God,
you are the Spirit of Truth;
lead me into all truth.

While I am growing in body
and enlarging the capacity of my mind,
enable me to grow more Christlike,
as a person of honesty
with deep respect for truth.

Increase my ability to separate
facts from fiction,
honest opinion from advertisement,
friendship from manipulation,
faith from superstition,
love from possessiveness.

Save me from simple trust in
all that newspapers print,
the fantasy world of *Cleo* and *Playboy*,
the gossip that is whispered to me,
the painted public face
and scripted words of TV stars,
or opinions which I'm not prepared
to test with people I trust.

Spirit of Truth,
lead me through the maze
of modern morals,
different religions,
society's many pressures,
and the selfishness in my own feelings.

This I ask in the name of him who saved me
for all that is beautiful, true, and loving.

Entertainers

God of joy, we thank you
for capacity to enjoy entertainment,
and for those with the skills to entertain us.
We are grateful for
those at the theatre,
in the concert hall,
in our malls and gardens,
or on TV,
who make us clap, cry,
think deeply, or laugh at ourselves.
Thank you for
clowns, singers, comperes,
actors, jugglers, dancers,
magicians and musicians.

Yet save us, God our Saviour,
from taking them too seriously.
Rescue us from treating the world of entertainment
as more real than the duties and joys of our own daily pilgrimage.
Free us from blind adulation
of art which does not glorify you.
Deliver our society from the sin
of turning entertainers into idols,
and from making their personal lives models for our values and goals.

Give us the grace
to have only one Model and one Lord,
for your love's sake.

Shepherd of Your Sheep

We come together, loving God,
in need of encouragement and correction,
confession, challenge, and assurance.
Give to each of us at least one moment of truth today,
when we may know that we are loved and treasured
by the Good Shepherd who knows his sheep by name.

Great Shepherd of the sheep,
let your peace rest on your world family,
that there may be an end of cruelty, anger, war,
persecution, injustice, exploitation, and alienation,
and the way of love begin to rule among all mankind.

Good Shepherd, we ask you this day
to tend your sick ones,
rest your weary ones,
feed your hungry ones,
soothe your suffering ones,
comfort your grieving ones,
pity your afflicted ones,
and rejoice with your joyful ones.*

In your mercy, deepen the hope of this congregation here gathered,
that the future may be faced in the spirit of Jesus Christ our Lord.

* St Augustine

Itinerant Workers

Most loving God,
you sent among us
an itinerant Preacher of no fixed address,
who by the paradox of grace
has opened up a new and living way
for us to be truly at home.

In his name we pray
for itinerant workers
who live rootless lives
so that we might enjoy life more.

We thank you for:
    roadbuilders and maintenance crews
    who live in grey camps beside our highways;
    teachers, clergy, bankers, railway workers,
    policemen, and others, who spend much of
    their lives without a home of their own;
    truckies who spend so many waking hours
    on the highways, away from home;
    itinerant fruit-pickers moving with the seasons
    from the Derwent Valley to Mildura,
    from Barossa to Coffs Harbour,
    from Nambour to Bundaberg.

We pray for the families of these oft-forgotten folk:
    the young people who spend life in caravan parks,
    constantly changing school and losing friends;
    wives who rarely see their husbands,
    and children for whom their father is like a stranger;
    the marriages which break
    under the strain of infrequent cohabitation;
    the mal-adjusted youngsters who have suffered
    emotional damage through constant insecurity.

Each of these wanderers
has a name which you know,
and a life which you treasure.
In your love, be with them
on their journeys
and support them in their crises:
through Jesus Christ, our way, truth, and life.

Small Country Towns

Country life has many joys, O God,
for which we give you thanks.
But when we drive through some towns,
we know that all is not well.

We pray especially for country towns
which are shrinking in size,
with townfolk demoralized and depressed
as old family businesses close,
and the paint on struggling shops
gets more faded and tatty.

We remember the many people
who have been compelled to move
far away from families to find work,
and the unemployed youth who drift
around the pubs and clubs.

We pray for country folk as
schools shrink,
community organizations peter out,
priests and ministers are withdrawn
to larger towns and parishes,
and medical care is reduced.

God, you treasure the people
of these shrinking towns.
Show them how to adjust
in creative ways.
Richly bless that small group of citizens
who struggle to maintain the essential services
and facilities of their communities.

Father of the Galilean,
Father of us all,
hear our prayers.

Children in Hospital

Loving Lord, you know the joys and fears of little children.
Bless your little ones who are in hospital today:
If they are in pain,
give them the strength to bear it with your help.
If they are afraid,
give them the courage to share it with those who nurse them.
If they are so ill that only parents are allowed to visit,
help them to understand they have not been deserted
by sisters, brothers, or friends.

Gentle Lord, help the doctors and nurses
to be gentle, sensitive, and reassuring.
When painful treatment must be administered,
give your children confidence and trust in those who give it.

Put a sweet soothing prayer in the souls of the youngsters
who are too weak or too young to pray for themselves.
Above all else, help them to know they are never alone.
When family or friends leave and kiss them goodnight,
when the lights are turned low and quietness descends,
let them know for sure that you are at their side,
cradling them in strong warm arms,
soothing their fears and filling them with love and peace.

This is our prayer, through Jesus,
who shared our childhood and knows our pain.

Bushfires

Loving God,
our prayers today are where our hearts and minds
have been during last week:
with the victims of the bushfires.

We pray for those who mourn their dead:

families, neighbours, schoolfriends, workmates.
O God, divine Friend,
be with them in their desperate sorrow.
Comfort their torn hearts
and heal them from nightmare memories.
Let there be joy,
let there be peace,
let there be hope,
let there be love.

We pray for the injured survivors in our hospitals:
Those who are severely burnt or disfigured,
and those suffering ones who may never recover.
Relieve them from pain, and soothe their tortured minds
by your Holy Spirit.
Let there be joy,
let there be peace,
let there be hope,
let there be love.

Gracious Lord, we pray for all who lost their homes:
Comfort them as they grieve the loss
of very special personal possessions,
treasured photos or letters,
gifts, heirlooms, or mementos
which held a host of precious memories.
Let there be joy,
let there be peace,
let there be hope,
let there be love.

We pray for the firemen who mourn dead comrades:
Be with them in their distress.
Bless their dedication and courage,
and stir our society to make sure they are provided
with the best facilities and safety equipment
for their vocation.
Let there be joy,
let there be peace,
let there be hope,
let there be love.

We pray for all those working for the rehabilitation of the victims:
The government, Red Cross, the church,
telephonists, social workers, pastors,
and a host of friends, neighbours, and generous citizens.
Give us the grace to help in ways which will respect human dignity,
speed recovery, and restore hope.
Let there be joy,
let there be peace,
let there be hope,
let there be love.
These prayers we ask through the One
Whose Spirit inspires our compassion, Jesus our Lord.

Forgotten People

God of all who labour
and are heavy laden,
awaken within us gratitude
for all the forgotten people
who work behind the scenes
and receive sparse thanks.

We pray for all
   cooks, cleaners and clerks,
   gardeners, garbage collectors and grave diggers,
   secretaries, street sweepers and sandwich makers,
   bakers, brewers and bee-keepers,
   drycleaners, designers and drovers,
   telephonists, traindrivers and typists.

We give thanks, O Lord,
for their loyalty and skill,
and pray that our community
may become more appreciative
of all who toil in the background
to enhance our daily lives.

This we pray
   in the name of the Lord
   who did not shrink
   from washing the feet
   of his followers.

Part VII
AS YOU LOVE YOURSELF
Be with us, Lord

Today in the City

Lord of all life,
Lord of each hour:
Be with us today.

At tram stop or bus station,
at roundabout or traffic light:
Be with us today.

On freeway or footpath,
on stairway or escalator:
Be with us today.

By assembly line or typewriter,
by kitchen sink or computer:
Be with us today.

In clamour or quietness,
in talk or in sickness:
Be with us today.

Among friends or competitors,
among atheists or believers:
Be with us today.

Lord of the beginning,
Lord of the ending:
Be with us today.

Hallowed be Your Name

Wonderful God,
wise beyond our conceiving,
loving beyond our feeling,
our Father by Christ's revealing:
Hallowed be your name.

Through our speaking and listening,
seeking and finding:
Hallowed be your name.

In our loosing and binding,
choosing and discarding:
Hallowed be your name.

By our caring and crying,
sharing and suffering:
Hallowed be your name.

For your Christ and his story,
your kingdom and glory:
Hallowed be your name.

In Spirit and Truth

Spirit of life,
your touch is pure grace,
more gentle than fingers of light,
more sure than arms of granite.

You caress our being
and awaken in us
a passion for more light,
more truth,
greater love.

You are kneading our spirit
with fingers of love
until faith
is no mere doctrine
but our autobiography.

Long Weekend

Lord of all our days,
today we are not finding it easy
to enter into worship with enthusiasm.
Many of our friends are on holiday,
and the congregation is sparse.
We are even a little envious
of the opportunity many have
for a change from the normal routines.
We feel apathetic,
and are in danger of infecting our worship
with a second-rate approach.

Loving God,
rescue us from apathy and envy.
Open our sluggish souls to your Spirit,
that we may awaken to the wonder
of being in your house on this Lord's Day.
Help us to count your mercies in Christ
rather than our absent friends.
Inspire us again
with the joy of this holy day.

Please bless our absent members.
Whether they are worshipping with another congregation,
or experiencing recreation in other ways,
may the life of the Risen One dwell in them.
Turn their holiday into a holy day.
Refresh us all for the ongoing tasks
and privileges of this new week.

Blessed be your name, O Lord.
To you all praise is due,
today and always.

Turn to Us

Lord our God, in the name of Jesus,
help us to break the hold
that failure and discouragement has upon our hearts:
To you, O Lord, we turn for encouragement;
turn to us and help us.

When our sins oppress us, and our spirits grow faint,
and the gloom of failure settles upon us,
help us to see through the shadows:
To you, O Lord, we turn for light;
turn to us and help us.

When we doubt the goodness of life
because evil and suffering blind us to life's goodness,
give us the grace to rise above despair:
To you, O Lord, we turn for grace;
turn to us and help us.

When we are tempted to suppress our deep longing
for goodness, and to deny our better selves,
re-awaken our souls:
To you, O Lord, we turn for renewal;
turn to us and help us.

When we become immersed in trivial pleasures
and material cares, forgetting you,
may the ordinary things of life
bear witness to your presence and goodness.
To you, O Lord, we turn in trust.
Blessed be your name, Saviour and Friend,
the Beginning and End.

Save Your Children

God, most holy and most compassionate,
save your children from the evil
which lies in wait even for your saints.
God of great mercy, we pray
that you will forgive us for our addiction
to words instead of deeds:
Lord, hear us and help us.

That you will rescue us
from our suspicion toward those
who attend a different church,
speak with a different accent,
or vote for a different political party:
Lord, hear us and help us.

That you will make us alert
to the silences or the cries
of those who are too weak
to defend themselves against injustice:
Lord, hear us and help us.

Please awaken our sensitivity
to those hidden fears
and self-dislike
which may make some people so unlovely:
Lord, hear us and help us.

That we may face up
to whatever embarrassment,
apology, or restitution is needed
to right the wrongs we have committed:
Lord, hear us and help us.

That, by the grace, mercy, and peace
of our Lord Jesus Christ,
you will enable us to say goodbye
to old shame, pessimism, and fear,
and be glad to accept your free forgiveness:
Lord, hear us and help us.

Father of Jesus and our God,
in a world of mistrust and ingratitude,
anxiety and miserliness,
we give you thanks for your abundant generosity
and your loyalty toward us:
through our Saviour Christ Jesus.

Shepherd Us

Most loving God,
you are the Shepherd God
who cares for us with an infinite compassion,
seeking to help even the smallest,
  weakest,
  and lowliest
  in your flock.

Grant to us, we pray,
the readiness to put ourselves
under your direction,
that in our weakness
we may have your divine support,
and in our strength
the wisdom to use our power
in ways that will not hurt others.

So shall we fulfil your purposes
declared in our Shepherd King,
Jesus Christ our Lord.

All who are Heavy Laden

In this era of conflicts
   and mountainous problems,
we know what it is to labour
   and be heavy laden.
You have called us to go out
   into all the world
and immerse all nations
   in the Gospel of divine love.
We have tried, Lord,
   and have become tattered and tired,
   despondent, even a bit cynical.
We, the heavy-laden,
   come to you, Lord,
needing your rest.

As the native hen nests
   in the clumps of tussocks
   at the edge of quiet waters,
so give us a nesting place
   in the quiet places of your kingdom,
that our hope may be renewed
   as your mothering Spirit broods over us,
protecting us through
   every dark night of the soul,
until morning comes again
   and we are renewed —
   as if born again —
to learn from you the holy way
   that leads to life
for all humanity.

Be with Us

Creator of the earth and heavens
Lord of the past, present, and future:
Be with us this day.

God of times and seasons,
of fresh life and growth,
and mellow times of fruitfulness:
Be with us this day.

God of hope and joy,
of the loving heart, the gentle spirit,
and the determined will:
Be with us this day.

God of hope and joy, God of the loving heart,
Father of our Lord Jesus Christ, and our God:
Be with us this day.

Peace of God

When my days become over-busy,
and I get hassled by too many worries:
Sweet Lord, give me your peace.

When my vision begins to fade,
and weariness infiltrates the soul:
Strong Lord, give me your peace.

When, disgusted by my own faithlessness,
I toss on my bed through the night:
Faithful Lord, give me your peace.

When worship becomes a routine,
and prayer has the taste of sawdust:
Renewing Lord, give me your peace.

When my hair turns grey above a wrinkled face,
and my energy is spent before the day is done:
Unfailing Lord, give me your peace.

When I'm retired from work with its joys,
and wonder what it means to grow older:
Nurturing Lord, give me your peace.

When my mind glimpses strange sights,
and my heart ceases to beat:
Deathless Lord, give me your peace.

For Deliverance

God of Jesus and our God,
we are grateful for all who come from east and west,
north and south,
to feast in your Kingdom:
We are thankful for Jesus who calls us together.

We are grateful for the various shades
of people and opinion,
age-groups and experience,
which make your church such a unique family:
We are thankful for Jesus who calls us together.

(Silent Meditation)

Merciful God,
from bitterness, oppression,
war and terrorism:
Deliver your people, Lord.

From a church-life so broad
that it has no conviction,
and a church-life so narrow
that it has no catholic spirit:
Deliver your people, Lord.

From hunger,
homelessness,
unemployment and injustice:
Deliver your people, Lord.

From corruption in governments,
police forces,
and public service:
Deliver your people, Lord.

From shyness in befriending,
panic in suffering,
loneliness in grieving,
and fear in dying:
Deliver your people, Lord.

That the kingdoms of this world
may be gathered
into your eternal kingdom:
Deliver your people, Lord.

Contemporary Wilderness

Lord of life abundant,
keep your church alert
  to the needs of our fellow-Australians
  who become hurt or lost
  in the wilderness of modern life.

Keep us alert
  to the over-sensitive person,
  who puts on a bold front
  but suffers behind the facade.

Keep us alert
  to the disabled or disfigured person,
  who may be suffering
  behind closed doors.

Keep us alert
  to the overworked person,
  weary and exhausted
  in body, mind, and spirit.

Keep us alert
  to the unemployed person
  who is feeling useless,
  rejected, frustrated, and angry.

Keep us alert
  to the bewildered person
  who is 'bushed' by life
  and needs encouragement and guidance.

Keep us alert
  to those facing difficult decisions,
  confronting serious surgery,
  or bearing heavy burdens.

Lord of the wilderness,
keep us alert also
to our own deep needs.
When our path becomes rough
or our thirst begins to burn,
give us not what we ask,
but what we truly need:
through Christ Jesus, our Lord.

Light

God of light,
let your light draw us nearer to you,
and to our neighbours in all the earth,
now and in generations to come —

Nearer to your generosity,
    and to all our hungry and homeless neighbours.
Nearer to your compassion,
    and to those who are broken in body, mind, and spirit.
Nearer to your righteous anger,
    and to people who suffer from mental or physical abuse.
Nearer to your comfort,
    and to those who sorrow because of death or alienation.
Nearer to your all-inclusive love,
    and closer to neighbours who have no faith or hope.
Nearer to your peace,
    and to all who are caught in destructive conflicts.

God of light,
continue to impregnate this grey and bewildered world
with your light,
that the glory of your final purpose
may find a joyous completion in us:
through Jesus Christ our Lord.

Renew Our Spirit

Deep is your love for us, O God.
Great is your compassion;
You have breathed a new spirit into us,
and your Spirit sustains it.

As long as I have breath,
I dedicate my being to you,
my skills and my gifts,
my joy and my love.

But I have failed to fulfil
my rich destiny as your Spirit's child.
I am not living or reflecting
the fulfilled life of Christ Jesus.

My failures are many,
my faults are obvious;
my faith falters,
and my love lapses.

Yet it is still my joy
to accept your forgiveness in Christ Jesus,
to bear witness to your love,
and to cling to your vision
of a new heaven and a new earth.

God most wonderful,
we place our longings for a nobler life before you,
and look to your abundant mercy:
through Jesus Christ our Lord.

Part VIII

FOR SHEPHERDS ONLY
Ministers, Pastors and Priests

New in the Parish

Living God,
thank you for the privileges
of being an ordained pastor
within your church.

For the honour of expounding
the Holy Bible
and the joy of celebrating Holy Communion:
I give you my gratitude.

For the favour and responsibility
of speaking your word of forgiveness
to broken spirits:
I give you my gratitude.

For the welcome
I receive as I move into a new parish,
and the respect, love, and trust so freely given:
I give you my gratitude.

For the pleasure
of invitations into homes,
and the fun of sharing a family meal:
I give you my gratitude.

For being allowed
to assist people
in their time of need:
I give you my gratitude.

For the wonder of witnessing
bushed and defeated folk
rediscover their faith and confidence:
I give you my gratitude.

For being supported
by those whom we support,
and blessed by those whom we bless:
I give you my gratitude.

I thank you for my calling,
and praise you for the grace
of my Lord, Jesus Christ.

Serving at Table

God most holy,
your love is awesome.

As I stand before
this holy Table,
I wish you had a celebrant
worthy to be here.

I am not worthy
to gather up the crumbs
from under your table,
but you have invited me
like an honoured guest.

That I should be your servant
in this Mystery,
causes me to tremble
with that unique fear
composed of awe and love.

May I discern
the presence of the Body
as I eat and drink of things divine,
lest, victim of familiarity,
I miss the Host,
though touching the gift.

Our Peculiar Temptations

God, you search me and know me;
save me from the peculiar temptations
to which a minister is exposed.

From allowing holy words and tasks
to become mere rite and habit:
Deliver me, O God.

From the lust for self-display
which feeds on public appearance:
Deliver me, O God.

From that bogus humility
which craves the reputation of being humble:
Deliver me, O God.

From allowing the expectations of parishioners
to shape haphazardly my attitudes and priorities:
Deliver me, O God.

From the unwillingness to recognize and use
the diverse skills of lay people:
Deliver me, O God.

From offloading to the laity
only those tasks I find distasteful:
Deliver me, O God.

From being unwilling to seek counsel
from other clergy or laity:
Deliver me, O God.

From the insecurity which makes me jealous
when other ministers seem more competent than I:
Deliver me, O God.

Lord of the Church,
give me the grace
to love these people
with whom I minister,
and to allow them
to love me.

Enigma

God, the name above all other names,
sometimes I think my name is Enigma:
Made in your image,
but sculptured from dirt;
Possessing your breath,
    but inhaling with infected lungs;
Owning Jesus as my true Brother,
    but also related to Judas and Pilate;
As clear as moonlight over frosty paddocks,
    but as muddy as a buffalo's wallow.

Yet, on my best days,
when the air is clear
    and the sun is shining,
my spirit hovers like a lark
    between earth and sky,
singing the loveliest melodies
    I have learnt on earth,
longing, longing to unite them
    with the music of the heavens.

O God, because you truly love
this human enigma,
and made me a member
of your family,
let me learn some notes
    with which angels praise you,
and grant me the grace to echo them
    amid the mundane stuff of life.
For your love's sake.

Bitter Cup

Today, Lord, I saw a mother take
her dying child
   from the hospital cot
   and enfold him in her arms.
   She mopped the little fevered face
   and when dry lips
   whispered 'Mummy'
   I saw a woman
   writhe in anguish
   unspeakable.

Today, Lord, I saw a father hold
his dead child
   in his arms
   and watched him
   place the little body
   back at last
   in the barren cot
   soundlessly,
   in the agony
   of raw grief.

Lord, I felt so wordless,
overwhelmed with grief
   for the grieving.
   The one true thing
   for me to do
   was to put arms around them
   and whisper the Word
   about a holy cross
   where you
   tasted the bitter cup,
   then lead them away
   from the ward.

Lord, at times
it is only that Word
which stands between
me and the nightmare
of utter despair.

One Minute before the Sermon

Holy God,
at this moment I am a little
awed and scared
just as I have been
a thousand times before.
I want this sermon to be
a holy experience
for these people and for me.

Yet I know
that my motives are mixed.
There is within me
one overwhelming desire
that as the preacher
I may be a nobody:
that the Gospel may be heard
and not the preacher.

But also in me
is another want:
to be a successful preacher,
just as at other times
I want to be
a successful pastor.

Please take
my mixed abilities and motives,
the love I have for you
and the love I have for myself,
and let them be welded
into one strong unity
by the fire of your Spirit.
Let the living Word
be heard,
through me,
or in spite of me.
Let all be to your glory!

PHOTO CREDITS

Cover Banksia prionotes, WA (I. Traeger)

Page
8 Pioneer farmhouse ruins, SA (P. Furnell)
13 Shearing the rams (J. Pohl)
18 River reflections (B. Grieger)
33 Riding the waves (G. Smith)
34 Standley Chasm at noon, NT (J. Hoopmann)
37 Surging flood-waters (J. Pohl)
49 Battered, but strong (J. Hoopmann)
53 St John's Church spire, Barossa Valley, SA
57 Sunrise (J. Sawade)
60 Billabong, west of Alice Springs, NT (I. Traeger)
65 Boats at dawn, Granite Island, SA (J. Pohl)
67 Toadstools (J. Pohl)
68 Wild flower, Badgindarra (J. Hoopmann)
72 Windmill (J. Pohl)
75 Cricket crowd (G. Smith)
77 Pelican, Coorong, SA (G. Smith)
85 Eucalypts, Central Australia (J. Gregor)
89 Sunset, Flinders Ranges, SA (L. Doubtfire)
91 Strolling in the park (G. Smith)
94 Fishing at Waitpinga, SA (J. Pohl)
96 Green glory (G. Smith)
104 Festival Theatre, Adelaide (Adelaide City Council)
109 Rundle Mall, Adelaide (Adelaide City Council)
113 Kangaroo and friends, Cleland Park, SA (J. Pohl)
115 Sturt pea, Flinders Ranges, SA (L. Doubtfire)
123 Aboriginal, Hermannsburg, NT (I. Traeger)
127 Aboriginal rock paintings, NT (B. Grieger)
135 Bushfire havoc, 1983 (J. Gregor)
141 Holiday peace (J. Pohl)
143 Reverie in the dusk (G. Smith)
147 Anthill near Pine Creek, NT (J. Hoopmann)

The following poems were included in the 2002 Openbook Publishers edition of *Australian Prayers.*

Like Opal Miners

God of all days, on this cloudy asphalt morning,
when even the birds sit desultory on dead tree limbs,
tune my heart to the infra-joy which underpins all.

Like opal miners, let me dig deep to find the splendour.
Like artesian water, release a gusher of gratitude.
Like inland flowers, festoon my spirit with praise.

God of all days, source of 'solid joys and lasting pleasures',
please give me a 'makeover' by your irrepressible Spirit,
and let praise shape all my words and actions.

Made for Light

In your presence, holy Creator, we celebrate the knowledge that
we are creatures who are made for the light:

> solar light: starlight over Uluru, moonlight on rolling ocean
> waves, dawn light over city towers, sunlight on mountain ridges;
> Christ light: Bethlehem light, Galilee light, cross light, and Easter
> light in churches, markets and our cemeteries;
> God light: true light, grace light, joy light, love light, most
> beautiful and everlasting kindly light.

Holy God, you have made us for yourself, and our light is
darkness till we find our light in you. Blessed is your name on
earth and in heaven.

Untamed Things

I thank you, God, for untamed things:
desert wombats and sea eagles,
billabong yabbies and mountain brumbies,
welcome swallows and great whales,
the risen Christ and the gift of faith.

Hope

Make our hope, loving God, as tall as the faith of Christ and as
deep as his love. Keep us amazed in a stable, adoring beneath a
cross, and jubilant by an empty tomb. With such a hope
possessing us, let us serve you boldly, efficiently and merrily; for
your love's sake.

Victorious

O God,
you raised up your true Son
    to crush evil and give us abundant life.
Grant that, filled with this gospel,
    we may seek the company of Christ Jesus,
so that in his nurturing friendship
    we also may become victors over all evil
and begin now the promised life of the ages.
This we pray in his name.

Christmas Eve Intercession

Our God, Immanuel, while we meet on this warm summer evening in fellowship and love, we pray for all those who are left out in the cold.
May the light of Bethlehem's greatest child touch every dark place and enter each cold and lonely heart.

For those who because of persistent hatreds, terrorism or war are far from the promise of peace and goodwill,
come, Immanuel, and help your servants complete the tasks of love and peace which you have launched.

For those who this night live is refugee camps, squat in derelict buildings or sleep in back alleys or on the park benches of our cities,
come, Immanuel, and aid all your lost and homeless children to find their true inheritance.

For those who are ill, at home or in hospital, for those who are diseased or maimed, and for the latest accident victims of our highways and streets,
come, Immanuel, and bring comfort and hope through the nurses and doctors who do your healing work this night.

For those grieving people who for the first time are facing a Christmas without a precious loved one at their side,
come Immanuel, and give to the grieving that deep soul-peace that no human voice or hand can offer.

For the church in every land, wherever it worships and works in peace, and especially where it endures under constant threat and persecution,
come Immanuel, and give all your people the assurance of your constant presence and your all-sufficient grace.

And now, holy friend, we pray for ourselves, that this Christmas may not pass in vain.
O Spirit of Christ, the very Word of God who became flesh, give each of us the will and the wisdom to back up our prayers with appropriate actions;
to your praise and glory. Amen.

Holy Week

God in Christ, reconciling this lost world, draw me close to your heart.

Tear me away from false gods and secular creeds. Bring me again to that awful Place of the Skull, where heaven and earth most truly meet.

Let me see the cross wherever I go: at Wilpena and Wollongong, Port Arthur and Perth, Katoomba and Toorak, Renmark and Randwick, Natimuk and Norwood, Gove and the Gold Coast, Cooktown and Chifley, Gin Gin and Glenelg.

Everywhere, let me stand vulnerable before the cross of Christ Jesus and encounter the fearful pain, mystery and unfathomable love of salvation.

Welcome me, everywhere and every day, into the wounded arms of reconciliation. Yours is the glory, now and forever.

Some Easter Thanks

With high spirits we eagerly thank you, Easter God,
that we have been raised up with Christ
and look for those things that are timeless.

We eagerly thank you for bringing life and immortality to light
    through the gospel.
We eagerly thank you for the glorious witness of our living Christ
    to your unfailing, overriding providence.
We eagerly thank you for the promise that we now share in the victory
    which Christ Jesus has won.
We eagerly thank you that
    grace is stronger than evil,
    mercy is larger than suffering,
    joy is greater than grief
    and love is mightier than death.

All our joyful thanksgiving and loving praise we bring to you,
holy friend, loving saviour, and glorious God of irrepressible
Easter, through Christ Jesus, our risen Lord.

A Litany for National Repentance

Whenever we treat Indigenous Australians with less than respect, choosing charity because it seems cheaper than justice,
Lord, have mercy on me a sinner,
and bring us back to the love-courage of Christ.

Whenever city people presume to look on the rural community as a whingeing minority, and whenever country people see all urban citizens as pampered fools,
Lord, have mercy on me a sinner,
and bring us back to the love-courage of Christ.

Whenever we close our borders to those victims of oppression who seek asylum, closing our ears to their weeping and our hearts to their suffering,
Lord, have mercy on me a sinner,
and bring us back to the love-courage of Christ.

Whenever men cling to old cultural practices which demean women, and whenever women treat all men with distrust and disdain,
Lord, have mercy on me a sinner,
and bring us back to the love-courage of Christ.

Whenever we see unemployed people as unpleasant statistics, to be a cause for concern only when an election is on the horizon,
Lord, have mercy on me a sinner,
and bring us back to the love-courage of Christ.

Whenever children are abused and neglected in their own homes, and whenever we shut our eyes to the sexual exploitation of children on the streets,
Lord, have mercy on me a sinner,
and bring us back to the love-courage of Christ.

Whenever we begin to accept without distress the high rate of youth suicide, shutting our minds to the causes of their sense of desolation,
Lord, have mercy on me a sinner,
and bring us back to the love-courage of Christ.

Whenever we spend more in gambling venues than on education and health, and whenever governments exploit gambling as a revenue source,
Lord, have mercy on me a sinner,
and bring us back to the love-courage of Christ.

Whenever the church becomes blended with the cultural norms
of the community, surrendering its calling to be seen as fools for
Christ's sake,
Lord, have mercy on me a sinner,
and bring us back to the love-courage of Christ.

Now, most holy friend, please take these prayers and let them
mingle with the gospel yeast which disrupts our flat lives and
transforms them into something remarkable and wholesome;
through Christ Jesus, our Saviour.

Thrice-personal God

Holy God, we know so little about you. Your dazzling light and
dark mystery are way beyond the reaches of our minds. So
whenever we get big-headed and pontificate about you, we are
being pathetically ridiculous.

Yet we delight in the few sure things we do know, those clues that
you have uncovered for us.

Father, Son and Holy Spirit, we adore you.
When we name you as Father, dark chaos and futility give way
to the light of providential pattern and purpose.
When we name you as the Son, sin and frustration are
swallowed up by resurgent grace and hope.
When we name you as Holy Spirit, our weariness and timidity
are expelled by the energy of intimate love.

Creator, Redeemer and Inspirer, we cling to you, we delight in
you, we want to be possessed by you now and forever. Yes, holy
God, now and forever.

Thanksgiving: Let Everything Thank God

Let our land and everything in it give thanks to God.

Clap your hands, you rainforests of the Daintree and Franklin.
  Sing for joy, you streams of Gippsland and New England.
  Shout thanks, you mountains of the Flinders and the Snowy.
  Give glory, you wildflowers of the West and the Red Centre.
  For God comes. Yes, the holy one comes to renew the earth,
  to turn its trials into gladness and its pain into triumph.

Clap your hands, you gentle wallabies and bilbies.
  Sing for joy, you magpies, wrens and lyrebirds.
  Shout thanks, you dingoes, kookaburras and koalas.
  Give glory, you wombats, lizards and brolgas.
  For God comes. Yes, the holy one comes to cherish your lives,
  to turn your fear into safety and your suffering into joy.

Clap your hands, you Aborigines and Asians.
  Sing for joy, you Europeans and Polynesians.
  Shout thanks, you children, parents and teachers.
  Give glory, you church congregations and pastors.
  For God comes. Yes, the holy one comes to take you from failures
  to victory and from brief pleasures to great joy.

Night Rain

After a drought, we thank you, God, for waking us in the night to the sound of rain on the roof.

At first the gentle patter, and the soft music of water trickling from the guttering. Then the heavier beating of an extravagant fall, with the downpipes gurgling.

For those precious minutes as we lie on our backs, listening, before drifting off into a very deep, contented sleep, we thank you, generous God.

With sheer grace you continue to send your rain on both the just and the unjust; which is just as well or we would miss out.

We praise your saving name; through our brother, Christ Jesus.

For the End of Terrorism

Most merciful God, friend and saviour, please help this world to rid itself of the obscenity of terrorism and of the greed and injustice which feeds its roots. In both affluent countries and in the impoverished ones, may your will be done. Among those whose culture is influenced by Islam or Buddhism, or among those who have been taught by Hindu faith or Christianity, let the thirst for justice, compassion and peace prevail over fear and hatred and avarice. Give us minds that are willing to be taught, goals that can be reshaped, desires that are purged, and wills that are toughened to seek the good of all through loving means. This we can only do with your help. On you we cast our fate; through Jesus Christ our Lord.

In the Good Times

Please God, encourage me, this common disciple of Jesus, to keep going forward; to keep the faith through these soul-testing times when life is sweet and easy.

I think I do OK in the sour and rough episodes, when every step is a great challenge. That is when the issues seem clear, my need of you is acute, and my prayers are urgent and vital. I admit I don't always get it right, but at least I know what I believe and the Christ I would die for.

But good times are more treacherous. My days have been comfortable, the views pretty, the company pleasant and the challenges minuscule. Things are so cosy that I wonder whether I am moving at all.

Don't get me wrong, holy friend. I'm not asking for troubles. It is just that I don't want to miss you while I am admiring the view, or lose the way while immersed in contentment. In these good times, keep me alert, that at your call I may be ready; for Christ's sake.

New Science

Holy friend, please keep my mind open to you. Do not tolerate any pious paranoia towards those secular discoveries which throw light on your ways.

Let each scientific disclosure enlarge my wonder at the awesome intricacy and the glorious enormity of your power and intimacy. From genetic codes to the big bang, may my curiosity abound and worship engulf my comprehension; through Jesus Christ our Lord.

Offertory Prayers

With frail human hands we bring our offering, loving God. We place it in your strong divine hands to be blessed and then translated by the hands of your church into ministries of love for this nation and world; through Christ, our Saviour.

Wonderful are you, Lord God of the universe! Out of the good earth you give us life and prosperity, unmeasured and bountiful. From among your many gifts, we bring these back to you with thanksgiving. May their wise use declare your glory; through Christ Jesus, our Redeemer.

Holy friend, your goodness has never been rationed or delivered with partiality; help us to learn this hard lesson from you. With these gifts of money receive also the treasure of our thoughts and feelings, abilities and skills, and all the best of our hopes and holiest dreams. We offer you our deepest and best; through Christ Jesus, our Saviour.

Gracious God, we offer you these gifts, which are in fact already yours. The cattle on a thousand hills are yours, the wealth of mine and factory are yours, and the harvest of cornfields and commerce is yours. Help us to be good stewards, ready to give account not from fear but from love; in the name of Christ Jesus, the best steward of them all.

Blessed are you, joy of the universe! You have been prodigal in creation, with abundance flowing and flowering everywhere. You have been even more prodigal in the gift of redemption, giving up your precious only Son for our healing. Please receive our adoring gratitude with these offerings placed on your table, and may the offering of our daily lives likewise speak your praise; through Christ our Lord.

Intercession: For Our Land and Its People

For the land
> Loving Creator, we pray for our wide island continent:
> its forests, deserts, rivers, billabongs and mountains, its
> coastlands, lakes, islands and seas, its unique marsupials and
> birds, its reptiles, fish, coral reefs, dugongs, turtles and great
> whales.
>
> *Loving Creator, forgive any neglect or abuse of our land. Make us*
> *wise stewards of this country, that our children's children may be*
> *able to delight in it as we do.*

For our people
> Loving Parent, whose likeness we share, bless our people.
> Bless Indigenous Australians and the most recent migrants.
> Bless the descendants of European settlers and convicts, the
> Asians, Pacific Islanders, and new refugees arriving from far
> lands.
>
> *Loving Parent of us all, forgive any intolerance. Enable us to*
> *treasure every face and race, to redress injustices, and to seek*
> *the common good for one and all.*

For our nation
> Loving Leader, give wisdom and grace to our nation. We pray
> for the prime minister and premiers, ministers, parliaments,
> councils and courts, for service organisations and welfare
> groups. We pray for those who represent us overseas:
> ambassadors, consuls, exchange students, athletes, tourists,
> aid workers, peacekeeping forces and missionaries.
>
> *Loving Leader, the only pure guide, forgive our political and*
> *social cynicism. Help our leaders to do justice, to love kindness,*
> *and to walk humbly with God.*

For the church
> Loving Pastor, please continue your ministry through the
> churches of this wide and diverse land.
> Bless the old denominations and the new, the rigid and the
> relaxed, the high church and charismatic, the small or large.
> Bless those worshipping in ornate stone churches and those
> in small weatherboard chapels, those in coastal cities and
> those in inland towns and provincial cities.
> Bless our own denomination, and all other congregations and
> parishes, committees, synods and assemblies.

An Aussie Confession

Great Creator, we tend to think that we are far superior to the animal kingdom, yet at times we are much like it and sometimes far below it.

Sometimes we are like wombats hiding in dark burrows rather than like people living in the light.
Sometimes we are like a flock of galahs, squabbling, chattering and screeching so much that we don't even hear the cries of the wounded or lost.

Sometimes we are like inquisitive emus, curious about the ways of Christ but quick to take fright and run.
Sometimes we are like bowerbirds, so busy collecting pretty possessions that we miss the greater wonders around us.

Loving Creator, generous Saviour, forgive both our inflated egos and our deflating behaviour. By the fierce love of Christ, rebuke, forgive, liberate and rearrange our lives.
Help us to walk in Christ's clear light, to recognise the needs of those around us, to put you first, and to treasure that costly love-light which is the very environment of heaven. In his name we pray. Amen.

The Word of Forgiveness
L: Those who wait for the Lord shall renew their strength. They shall mount up with wings like eagles. They shall run and not be weary. They shall walk and not faint. Christ Jesus is risen and goes on ahead of you. In him you are a forgiven and renewed people.
P: Thanks be to God.

PART III

Never Alone

Never Alone

has been reproduced
from the
1984 Palm Tree Press Edition.

Contents

Part 1   Come, Advent God

Come, Advent God   11
Preparation   12
Come, Lord Jesus   12
The Word within the
    Word   14
Prepare the Way   15
He comes   17
Christmas confessions   18
Emmanuel   19

Remembering the Needy   20
Gloria in Excelsis   21
Your Day   22
Incarnation   22
Contradictions   23
The Leap Forward   24
New Year's Eve   25
Searching and Finding   27

Part 2   Not by Bread Alone

Lent   31
The Way of the Cross   32
Not by Bread Alone   33
Don't Tempt God   34
Don't Test God   35
One Lord   37
The Lost   38
From the Depths   39

Following in His Ways   40
Healing   41
He Who comes   42
Jesus is King   43
Hosanna   44
Forsaken?   45
The Suffering Servant   46
Good Friday   48

Part 3   Astounding God

Astounding God   51
The Divine Secret   52
Easter   53
Christ is Risen   55
Christians Together   56
Trusting New Life   57
On the Rays of the
    Morning   57

The Right-hand Man   58
Our God   59
Jesus   60
Reflection of the Unseen   62
Transforming
    Misfortunes   63
Grace of Our Lord
    Jesus Christ   64

Part 4   Life in the Spirit

Life in the Spirit	67	Who Am I?	81
The Bountiful God	68	Touch and Heal Us	82
Transfiguration Day	70	Good to be Alive!	83
Holy Spirit, Help us	71	Save Your Children	84
City Pentecost	72	Planting True Vines	85
Special People	73	The Still Centre	86
The Body	74	God's Strength	87
Holiness	75	Faith, Hope and Love	88
For Those who Hunger	77	Enigma	89
Hunger and Thirst	78	Happiness	90
For the Affluent	80		

Part 5   Never Alone

Such a Strange Mixture	93	The Only Hope	102
When	94	Unspeakable Joys	103
Familiar Things	95	A Quiet Spirit	103
For Things that Go Well	96	Dependable Word	104
Exuberant Praise	97	Hurry and Worry	105
Morning Sunlight	98	Never Alone	106
Daybreak	99	Our Work	107
This New Day	99	Joys of Home Life	108
Shame and Glory	100	Homes	109
Faith	100	Children in Hospital	110
Divine Generosity	101	Happy People	111
As Eagle and Dolphin	101	Good Shepherd	112
The Word and the		Thanksgiving for Light	113
Babble	102	Evening Prayer	114

Part 6   Come Quickly!

Father of the Lights	117	Come Quickly	121
The Ways of God	118	Judgment	122
A New Song	119	Endless Love	123
All Souls	120	His Arms	124

Introduction

The God I worship is everywhere.

We are never alone in this life. Certainly we may feel alone at times, or shout a protest to the heavens that for some reason we have been deserted. But it is not true. He is with us in all situations and at all times. In worship or at work, in the fields or in factories, the Holy One is with us.

The 'sacred' and the 'secular' are our categories, not God's. Maybe we need such categories to simplify our use of language, but we should never regard them as a description of reality. The Holy One can reveal himself in the most ordinary situation or withhold disclosure in the most lofty religious activity. Either way, he is with us. With sovereign freedom the 'Spirit blows where it will'.

I would be the first to admit that some places and situations seem more conducive than others: under the willows by a stream on a summer's day appears more likely than in peak hour traffic on a grey winter's morning. Yet there are thousands under the willows who have no thought or perception of God, while some in peak hour traffic do achieve significant times of worship. The art of finding God (or should it be 'of allowing him to find us'?) has much to do with the whole orientation of one's life: finding the Lord in tough situations needs a combination of faith, grit and gift. Be sure of this, the Holy One is there for those who seek him in 'spirit and in truth'. He is to be found everywhere.

A warning: To worship God everywhere runs the risk of worshipping him nowhere. The 'everywhere' is only meaningful when it is constituted by numerous little 'somewhere's. I hope this volume of prayers and psalms which are coloured by many of my little 'somewhere's', will prove a help to others who seek to trust and worship the God who is everywhere.

Bruce D. Prewer

Part One

Come, Advent God

Come, Advent God

Come, Advent God,
and complete the special work of love
which you began in Jesus of Nazareth.

Many are cast down with spiritual needs,
thirsting for the peace of your forgiveness
and the warmth of your healing love.
Come to them with the grace they desperately need.
At evening or midnight, morning or midday,
Come, Lord Jesus.

Many are in despair through physical hardship,
seeking relief from their burdens
and hope in the midst of their cares.
Come to them with the help they desperately need.
At evening or midnight, morning or midday,
Come, Lord Jesus.

Many have minds and souls filled with hatred,
lives shackled by prejudice and terrible obsession
in Northern Ireland, the Middle East, Africa,
South America, Asia, and in our own Australia.
Come to them with the conversion they so desperately need.
At evening or midnight, morning or midday,
Come, Lord Jesus.

Your church in all the world also needs saving
from everything that threatens its mission.
Where it is persecuted, keep it faithful.
Where it persecutes, rebuke it.
Where it is seduced by affluence, shake it to its foundations.
Where it is self-satisfied, thoroughly unsettle it.
Where it is weak, poor, and meek, bless it with your joy, peace
and strength.
At evening or midnight, morning or midday,
Come, Lord Jesus.

Come, Advent God,
and complete your work in Jesus Christ,
through whom we offer these prayers.

Preparation

This is the season of His coming;
Night is far gone, the day is at hand.

It is time to wake from sleep;
**For the Son of Man comes at an hour
we do not expect.**

His coming is the advent of saving love.
Come, Lord Jesus.

His coming is good news for the poor,
freedom for captives, sight for the blind,
liberty for the oppressed,
and acceptance for the unacceptable.
Come, Lord Jesus.

Then shall the lame man leap like the hart,
and the tongue of the dumb sing for joy.
O come, O come, Emmanuel.

Come, Lord Jesus

'Come, Lord Jesus.'
'Come!' say the Spirit and the Church.
'Come!' let each hearer reply.
This same Jesus,
whom we love but no longer see,
shall come again in glory
to judge the living and the dead.
    Come, Lord Jesus.

Unexpected as a thief,
unexpected as a midnight guest,
unexpected as the lightning:
    Even so come, Lord Jesus.

To expose the hidden guilt,
to expose the schemes of men,
to expose the powers of darkness:
    Even so come, Lord Jesus.

Bringing judgment to the arrogant,
bringing discipline to the unfaithful,
bringing rebuke to the apathetic:
    Even so come, Lord Jesus.

Giving rest to the weary,
giving healing to the sick,
giving forgiveness to the repentant:
    Even so come, Lord Jesus.

Like light in darkness,
like water for the thirsty,
like a bridegroom for a bride:
    Even so come, Lord Jesus.

As the stiller of storms,
as the giver of living bread,
as the friend of sinners:
    Even so come, Lord Jesus.

With a kingdom for the poor,
with a world for the meek,
with rejoicing for the persecuted:
    Even so come, Lord Jesus.

Fulfilling the prayers of martyrs,
fulfilling the work of the cross,
fulfilling the resurrection joy:
    Even so come, Lord Jesus.

The Word within the Word

Most wonderful God, this is your world,
the fruit of your creating and redeeming word;
the word which shaped the history
out of which the Bible was written.

> For the Word from the beginning
> speaking as One who has authority,
> word of life:
> we thank you, Lord most high!

You spoke through many writers —
some simple and some sophisticated,
poets, historians, shepherds, and princes —
each inspired to pass the word on.

> For the Word which is a lamp,
> guide to our feet, beacon on our path,
> word of light:
> we thank you, Lord most high!

The scribes of many generations who toiled,
patiently reproducing the sacred scrolls,
you nurtured, God of the ages.
Through them your treasure came down to us.

> For those who delighted in your Word
> and forgot not your laws,
> word of truth:
> we thank you, Lord most high.

Translators you gave us, servants of the Word,
conveying the Good News in our native tongue;
Bede, Wycliffe, and the sages of King James,
Moffatt, Phillips, and scholars of today.

> For the Word that cannot be bound,
> skilfully spoken in due season,
> word like fire:
> we thank you, Lord most high.

Wonderful God, we rejoice in the Gospel,
the witness of the Bible to Jesus Christ,
the Word within the words,
speaking a saving word to all people.

    For the Word made flesh,
    glorious Word who dwells among us,
    word of love:
    we praise you, Lord most high.

Prepare the Way of the Lord

There is a voice that cries in the wilderness,
the prophet word demanding change:
'Prepare the way of the Lord;
fill in the gullies, level the ridges,
straighten the crooked, move the mountains.
God's glory shall be revealed
and every eye shall see it.'

    Smooth the rough places,
    move the mountains;
    let God's glory be displayed!

In the wilderness of our cities,
furrowed by freeways and shaded by skyscrapers,
where hollow people jostle without love
or get lost in the wastes of suburbia,
where anonymous persons hide in flats,
or broken men queue up at hostels
for a bed and respite from dereliction:
Prepare the way of the Lord.

    Smooth the rough places,
    move the mountains;
    let God's glory be displayed!

In the wilderness of our schools and colleges,
the training-ground for survival of the fittest,
where the young learn almost everything
except how to become children of God,
expanding in mind but not in soul;
where young people earn diplomas, but little wisdom,
or graduate with honours in all but love:
Prepare the way of the Lord.

Smooth the rough places,
move the mountains;
let God's glory be displayed!

In the wilderness of our politics,
a field of stones and shabby fame,
where some blatantly offer election bribes
or have the gall to say they're the greatest,
where caring members can get mauled by power-brokers
and are relegated to the back benches
till cynicism breeds like a horrible virus:
Prepare the way of the Lord.

Smooth the rough places,
move the mountains;
let God's glory be displayed!

In the wilderness of our religions
where theological fashions come and go,
buildings and crowds persist as status-symbols,
and pomp and circumstance are high on the ratings,
where evangelism can be considered poor taste,
prayer and sacrifice as optional extras,
and even Jesus is feared as 'extremist':
Prepare the way of the Lord.

Smooth the rough places,
move the mountains;
let God's glory be displayed!

Voice in the wilderness, what shall we do?
Prophet of the Lord, what is the word?
'Turn, turn, turn to the Lord;
you who have two suits, give to the naked;
if you eat well, share with the hungry;
in business and authority, deal with compassion —
and be ready for the One who comes with fire.'

Smooth the rough places,
move the mountains;
let God's glory be displayed!

He Comes
Psalm 24

He comes to his own world,
    though his own will not receive him.
Everything already belongs to him
    and the people of every nation.
From sea to sea he created it;
    all living things are his joy.

Can any of us dare face him?
    Or keep our poise in his presence?
If our hands had never harmed another,
    if our motives were perfectly pure,
If we had never been seduced by vanity,
    if no trace of deceit lingered in us,
Then we would boldly receive him,
    confidently seeking his blessing.

Corrupt we all are, yet we seek him;
    our generation searches for a god.
We are creatures who are always restless,
    seeking elusive security and peace.
We look for his face in our heroes;
    vainly we search in our libraries.

Lift up your tired heads!
    Open up your weary eyes!
The King of glory comes among us;
    he enters the gates of our humanity.
Who is this King of glory?
    The Lord who stoops to conquer,
The Lord of Shepherds and poor men,
    he is the King of glory!

Lift up your tired heads!
    Open your weary eyes!
The King of glory comes to you.
    Who is this King of glory?
The Lord of countless hosts,
    he is our King of glory!

Christmas Confession

If we have arrived at a time in our lives
when the Christmas story no longer
excites or renews us:
Have mercy upon us, O God.

If, in the midst of the riches of the Gospel
of Jesus Christ, we live like paupers:
Have mercy upon us, O God.

If the life of Jesus fails to challenge us,
or his death and resurrection cease to comfort us:
Have mercy upon us, O God.

If, in the face of the world's great need,
we hoard the Gospel like misers:
Have mercy upon us, O God.

(Silent meditation)

So that we may be forgiven and renewed:
Restore to us the joy of salvation.

So that we may be a loving community:
Restore to us the joy of salvation.

So that we may clothe our good intentions
with the garments of action:
**Restore to us the joy of your salvation,
through Jesus Christ our Lord.**

Emmanuel

God, in your grace and mercy,
you gave us your Son to be our Emmanuel;
give us a renewal of faith and life at this Christmas time,
and save us from our myths and evasions.

When we trivialize the Christmas Gospel:
Lord, have mercy.
When we talk of peace and goodwill,
with so little of it in our own lives:
Lord, have mercy.
So that we may not only sing carols and light candles,
but also serve the Christ
and allow the light to shine in and through us:
Lord, have mercy.

We thank you,
most generous God,
for all the peace and joy
which you give us.
**We thank you
for sins forgiven,
hope renewed,
relationships repaired,
faith rekindled,
for your great love in Jesus Christ
established once again in our lives.**

Jesus, our Emmanuel,
God with us,
we worship you
and joyfully offer the praise
of heart, voice, mind, and strength.

Remembering the Needy at Christmas

Lord, on this wonderful day we pause
to remember the needy people of this world
whom Jesus came to save:
May the light of his star touch every dark place.

As we meet in fellowship and goodwill,
we pray for the end of war and terrorism
in your torn world, especially...
As we eat, drink, and are merry,
we pray for the hungry, homeless, and diseased:
Bring them your compassion and justice, Lord.

As we enjoy being relaxed and happy today,
we remember the sick,
the lonely, the frightened,
the anxious and the sorrowing:
Bring them your comfort and peace, Lord.

As we prepare to leave this place of prayer
to go our separate ways,
we remember those friends and loved ones
who are not with us this Christmas:
Give them the assurance of your presence, Lord.

As we pass other churches,
we remember other denominations,
praying especially for those
we fail to understand or appreciate:
Fill them with Christmas joy and praise, Lord.

O Word made flesh,
give us the will and capacity
to embody our prayers
in compassionate and courageous deeds:
Fill us with the joy of service.

God in the highest, worthy of glory,
hasten the day
when the song of the angels shall find perfect fulfilment:
In the name of your incarnate Son, Jesus.

Gloria In Excelsis

1. Yours is the glory:
   Light in the word
   Word in the silence
   Warmth in the cold
   Life in the cell
   Love at the threshold.
   Yours is the glory
   Beginning and end.

2. Yours is the glory:
   Light over Eden
   Dust standing tall
   Praying and crying
   Loving and losing
   Laughing and sighing.
   Yours is the glory
   Beginning and end.

3. Yours is the glory:
   Light over Bethlehem
   Laughter in Nazareth
   Sunshine through Galilee
   Gloom in Gethsemane
   Cloud over Calvary.
   Yours is the glory
   Beginning and end.

4. Yours is the glory:
   Light from a tomb
   Love new arising
   Greeting and mending
   Renewing indwelling
   Trusting and sending.
   Yours is the glory
   Beginning and end.

5. Yours is the glory:
   Light in community
   People enlivened
   Liberated and caring
   Body of Jesus
   Impudent and daring.
   Yours is the glory
   Beginning and end.

Your Day

Jesus, how strong
and irrepressible
is this your day.

Though hedged by greed
and masked by tinsel,
it has its say.

Our crowds disperse
and turn tired eyes
to where you lay.

Some spurn the sign.
Rapt, others find God
in human clay!

Incarnation

Almighty God,
you have wonderfully created us,
and even more wonderfully saved us
through the holy incarnation.
Grant, we pray,
that, as Jesus completely shared our nature,
we may increasingly share his spirit
and live to your glory,
and thus inherit the life abundant
which you have prepared for us
in and through Jesus Christ our Lord.

Contradictions

God of vast generosity,
   your love planned the birth of the Baby
   who is born to save his people from their sins:

We confess to you and to each other,
   that, in this world of contradictions,
   we stand in need of your saving.

Forgive us
   if in the Christmas season we have used holy words
   in a shallow way,
   if we have conducted hollow celebrations,
   if we have given gifts only to those who give to us.

Forgive us
   if we have feasted without thanksgiving,
   caroled without joy,
   greeted without caring,
   and prayed without love.

May the living Word which has come to us —
   Emmanuel who is with us,
   Elder Brother who is one of us —
save us from our sins,
quieten us with his peace,
and fill us with his Spirit.

We delight to call his name Jesus,
for he is saving us from our sins.

The Leap Forward

Lord, shall Christmas come again
distracting us momentarily
from the boasts and myths
of that Babel we call civilization,
giving us a few days playing
at worshipping the Mystery —
before we rush back
to the world of contemporary fantasy
where diseased minds pretend
the real action is?

Lord, the things we laud as progress,
and name as giant steps forward,
are only the fancy footwork
of those who dance on the same spot,
dazzling the eyes that look on
with smart improvisations —
until we fail to see
how little we step forward
and how rarely we leap.

Lord, yours is the only advance.
That potent Bethlehem gift
is a tiny, weak thing
unable to walk, stand, or even sit —
yet in the hour of birth
leaping forward over ages,
and inviting us to follow
in this new and holy way
where even our few steps forward
release joy among herald angels.

Lord, now dawns our day of progress!
Little son of God, laid in a manger,
we adore your coming!
Now God is our image, of our flesh and blood!
You are our Saviour and brother
who lies in a cot.
You lie in our misery,
share all our needs,
and assure us of glory!
Hallelujah!

New Year's Eve

Lord of all our days,
be with us tonight,
when the car horns hoot,
church bells ring,
crowds shout and cheer,
and 'Auld Lang Syne'
is sung at numerous parties.

Let those of us who love you
celebrate with as much joy
but with more purpose than
those who love you not.

Put a new song of faith
on our lips,
and renew the optimism of grace
within our mind and heart:
through Christ our Lord.

God of the old year
which is passing away,
we commend to your mercy
those who are glad to finish this year.

We lift up before you
those who have critically overworked,
those who had no opportunity to work,
folk whose health has broken up,
or whose career has been shattered;
our neighbours who have tasted grief,
or who have contracted terminal illness;
people who will end this year homeless,
and those who end it in hunger or thirst.

God of the new year
which is dawning,
we also commend to your mercy
those who enter the new year eagerly.

We hold up before you
all who will take up new work,
or who will retire from work;
all who plan to be married,
or who look forward to parenthood;
the people who will buy their own home,
or who will commence at universities;
those who will come to faith in you,
and all whose faith will grow stronger.

God of the past, present
and the limitless future,
bless all your people,
that, set free from old fears
or shallow optimism,
we may live with the joy
of the children of God.

Searching and Finding

Most loving God,
who put it into the mind of the Wise Men
to search for Jesus,
please give to us the wisdom to seek and to find.

When we become proud and stubborn,
give us the wisdom to find our humble Lord,
born in a stable.

When we become bewildered and lost in life's rush,
give us the wisdom to find ourselves
in the light that streams from Bethlehem.

When we become selfish and covetous,
cluttering our lives with possessions,
give us the wisdom to find that the best joy lies
in offering our treasures to Christ.

When we become depressed by our human failures and sin,
give us the wisdom to find the divine compassion and mercy,
the forgiveness which Jesus came to bring,
enabling us to name him Saviour from personal experience.

God of the Wise Men and our God,
put into our minds the wisdom
to follow the star which leads us to Jesus Christ,
and to follow him, come what may,
till our travelling days are done
and you call us home.

Part Two

Not by Bread Alone

Lent

O come, let us return unto the Lord:
For he will have mercy and abundantly pardon.
The Kingdom of heaven is at hand;
repent and believe the Gospel:
His will is our peace.
His discipline is our hope.
His service is perfect freedom.
In his presence is fullness of joy.

You cannot live by bread alone:
Lord, have mercy.
You shall not test the Lord your God:
Christ, have mercy.
You shall worship the Lord God,
and him only shall you serve:
Lord, have mercy.

O God, we are so immersed in the materialism of our age
that we find it hard to recognize our sins:
Open our eyes to see ourselves as you see us.
Expose the secret gods within us,
pinpoint the deceits that blur our perception,
unmask the poverty of our souls,
expose our greed, arrogance, or apathy,
save us from our love of things and use of persons,
deliver us from morbid guilt, cheap discipleship,
and sentimental religion:
through Jesus Christ who suffered and died for us.

The Way of the Cross

**If anyone wants to come with me, he must forget self,
take up his cross every day, and follow me.** Luke 9:23 (TEV)

Lord, this is a troublesome saying,
  heavy and hard.
We jealously protect our gains,
  always on guard.
The more we have the more we crave,
  success self-made.
When you speak of losing all,
  we are afraid.

Lord, this is an embarrassing saying
  for folk like us.
Even over the smallest disciplines
  we make a great fuss.
We are not made of the stuff of heroes,
  without complaints.
We are just your little people,
  not noble saints.

Lord, this is a persistent saying,
  giving no rest.
In mind and soul we know it is sane,
  offering the best.
By gaining and grasping we know we lose
  life's deeper scope.
The strange logic of your cross remains
  life's only hope.

Lord, this is a saving saying,
  divine outlay.
The path of the cross the only glory
  all the way.
Willing, though fearful, help us to bear it,
  not growing slack.
Laughing and crying, help us to follow,
  not turning back.

Not by Bread Alone

Man cannot live on bread alone, but needs every word that God speaks. Matthew 4:4 (TEV)

I do have faith, but not enough. Help me to have more Mark 9:24 (TEV)

In a world where people live for pride,
eating the bread of vanity:
from the conceit that looks for public
    praise and honours;
from the vainglory that flaunts diplomas
    and degrees;
from the arrogance of religious and
    moral swagger;
from the insolence of supposed racial
    superiority,
save your children, Lord.

In a world where people live by force,
eating the bread of power:
from all attempts to manipulate
    our friends;
from the temptation to scorn a
    defeated opponent;
from the desire to use chance advantages
    to disadvantage others;
from leaders who love to rule
    more than to serve,
save your children, Lord.

In a world where people live by greed,
eating the bread of cupidity:
from envy of those
    with larger homes;
from selling our ethics
    for a few more dollars;
from trusting the stock-market
    more than the Scriptures;
from supporting only those charities
    which offer an income tax deduction,
save your children, Lord.

In a world where people live by pleasure,
eating the bread of sensuality:
from turning food
    into an extravagant habit;
from cluttering our homes
    with technological toys;
from using our sexuality
    for indulgent lust;
from loving things
    and using people,
save your children, Lord.

Don't Tempt God
Psalm 82

God takes a stand in the council of heaven,
    to judge those who live like gods.

How long will you encourage injustice,
    and give benefits to evil men?
You should lift up the weak and the orphan,
    give rights to all downtrodden people.
You should rescue the weak and the poor,
    freeing them from the grip of exploiters.
But you do not want to know,
    you are not willing to understand;
You stroll in the darkness
    while the foundation of the world shakes!

I tell you, though you could be godlike,
    children of the Most High,
You shall soon die like all men,
    you shall fall like all proud men.

O God, take your stand and judge us!
    The nations are at your disposal!

Don't Test God

The scripture also says, 'Do not put the Lord your God to the test'. Matthew 4:7 (TEV)

You must not test the Lord your God,
    nor ask for a sign of his presence;
His commandments are already given,
    guide-posts on the road to life.
His sign is imbedded in our history,
    the child of a young woman — Immanuel.
Only a wicked and perverse generation
    dare seek a greater sign than this.

Christ-given signs of his presence are with us:
    the haunted eyes of the starving
    looking at the camera of the tourist,
    and the pitiful band of refugees
    through whom Christ cries to us.
    As we sit at plenteous tables,
    or sleep in secure comfort,
    should we ask for other signs?
    Dare we test the Lord our God?

His signs are in our hospitals:
    thousands of road-accident victims,
    some dying, but not quickly enough,
    and many with no future
    except wheelchairs, callipers, or mindless years.
    Dare we test the Lord our God
    by saying prayers
    and then driving carelessly
    on our streets and highways?

The signs are in our churches:
    ordinary people with simple faith
    who humbly extend themselves
    with an extraordinary compassion
    in a thousand little actions;
    the unpretentious, grass-roots love
    which asks for no reward.
    Dare we test the Lord our God
    by demanding signs more grand?

Precious signs are in the Supper:
    fruits of our toil and the generosity of God;
    where the grace of soil, rain, and sunshine
    condense in a chalice
    and a piece of daily bread;
    where people meet with an everloving Host.
    Dare we test the Lord our God
    by asking for signs more profound?

One Lord
Psalm 33

If you are joyful, show it to the Lord!
    Stand tall and praise him!
Let music tell your gratitude:
    organ and guitar, trumpet and drums.
Haven't you a new song to sing?
    Put your whole strength into it.

What the Lord tells you is true;
    whatever he does is dependable.
He has a passion for integrity and justice,
    and sufficient love to fill the world.
Happy our nation when the Lord is God,
    when our people respond to his call.

The universe was framed from his words;
    the galaxies are his thoughts.
All the oceans are his waterbag,
    the Indian and Tasman his finger-bowl.
Let everything tremble before the Lord,
    every person stand in awe!

He scatters the diplomacy of empires;
    the Lord foils the schemes of the cunning.
Nations are not saved by vast armies,
    nor soldiers by brute strength.
Tanks and rockets don't give safety;
    no one wins by military power.

The purposes of the Lord are infinite;
    his plans extend from age to age.
Intimately he shapes the life of all,
    and broods over every single soul.
He is well aware of those who honour him;
    those who put all hope in his free grace.

Come, everyone! Let us place our hope in him!
    Let us love our helper and guardian.
Every fibre of our being rejoices in him,
    trusting his healing name.
Lord, let your sure love reside with us,
    for we have no hope or joy but you.

The Lost

The Son of Man came to seek and to save the lost. Luke 19:10 (TEV)

Lord, we get lost so easily:
    in the course of conversation,
    at the house of a neighbour,
    with good advice on our lips,
we get lost in our wisdom
and lose the gift of truth.

Lord, we get lost so unexpectedly:
    in the hour of success,
    at the home of a friend,
    with hymns on our tongues,
we get lost in our importance
and lose the gift of joy.

Lord, we get lost so crudely:
    in the middle of our prayers,
    at the party or the club,
    with humour in our words,
we get lost in our adaptability
and lose the gift of peace.

Lord, we get lost so profoundly:
    in the cause of Christian duty,
    at the social justice meeting,
    or with consecrated bread in our hands,
we get lost in our righteousness
and lose the gift of love.

Lord, we are found so simply:
    in the moment of awareness,
    at the hour of taking stock,
    with hunger in our being,
we lose ourselves in grace
and find the gift of life.

From the Depths
Psalm 130

Out of deep anguish I cry to you, Lord;
   Lord, can you hear me?
To the groaning of my prayers
   please carefully listen.
If you, Lord, keep a record of sins,
   then none of us dare face you.
But in you we find forgiveness,
   therefore we can adore you.
I wait, with all my soul I wait,
   and hope for the word I need.
With all my soul I long for my Lord,
   more than night-watchmen waiting for dawn.
Like the weary looking for sunrise,
   let all God's people wait in hope.
For with the Lord there is pure love,
   with him is abundant liberty.
He alone can set us free
   from all our sins.

Following in His Ways
Psalm 25

Our Lord, on you I rest my very being;
   on you I stake my life.
Don't let me ever be ashamed,
   or discouraged by the success of opponents.
No person who follows you is disgraced —
   only those who are unfaithful.

Show me, Lord, the disciple's path;
   teach me your ways.
Saviour, lead me and coach me;
   every day I'll trust your saving love.
Remember your unfailing compassion,
   shown throughout the ages.

Recall not the faults of my youth;
   remember me in your saving grace.
You alone are good and true;
   therefore show wanderers the way to go.
You guide ordinary folk aright;
   you teach the timid your way.

Lord, your loving ways are sure
   to those who follow and obey.
Your purpose is shown to true worshippers,
   and we experience your covenant.
I keep my eyes on you always;
   only you can save my feet from trouble.

When I feel lonely or depressed,
   Lord, turn back and encourage me.
If I grieve within my heart,
   free me from my distress.
When you see my anxiety and doubt,
   forgive my every sin.

Healing
Psalm 51

In your dependable love, Lord, I find healing;
   your unconditional acceptance removes my shame.
I want to be washed clean,
   to be made like new again.
Excuses for my sins are no good;
   my failure to love stands out a mile.
Worst of all, my lovelessness hurts you;
   what I fail to do for others adds to your pain.
When I think of you suffering,
   I quite justly feel most miserable.
But you don't hold it against me;
   you help me recover from my shame.
Lord, I want to be remade deep down;
   the current of life in me needs transforming.
Lord, my feelings need purifying;
   my attitudes and ideas must be reshaped.
Above all things, Lord, don't ever leave me;
   nor remove your saving Spirit from me.
Help me to delight in you more than anything else;
   in the liberty you give, may I stand up straight.

He Who Comes

Hosanna! Blessed be the King who comes in the name
of the Lord:
Hosanna in the highest!
If we should hold our peace, the very stones would
shout aloud:
Hosanna in the highest!

God of the King
who humbly rides on a donkey,
we who are conceited about our image and status,
need your salvation:
Come, Lord, save us.
God of the pilgrims
who publicly confessed their enthusiasm for Jesus,
we, who are embarrassed by public displays of faith,
need your salvation:
Come, Lord, save us.
God of the hesitant
who watched the holy procession,
but were in two minds about joining it,
we, who often falter in our convictions,
need your salvation:
Come, Lord, save us.

Gracious God, we thank you
for the experience of forgiveness
and the sense of your presence:
**We praise your grace in Jesus Christ,
who makes disciples out of sinners,
and creates new life in tired or barren lives.**

Hosanna! Blessed be the mercy
which comes in the name of the Lord:
Hosanna in the highest!

Jesus Is King

Come, join to praise with morning light:
  Our loving King!
Let grateful voices sound with might:
  Our loving King!
Let children's voices tell their praise,
While aged lips extol your ways,
Let every tongue in joy unite:
  Our loving King
  To you we bring
  Our praise!

Let songs like this ring through our land:
  Our loving King!
From coastal farms and inland sand:
  Our loving King!
Let all our nation thankful raise
Its voice in glad tumultuous praise:
  Our loving King
  To you we bring
  Our praise!

Let earth's great millions thund'rous shout:
  Our loving King!
Let this song spin the clouds about:
  Our loving King!
We'll always shout and sing your praise
While years flit by like passing days,
Until time runs its last hour out:
  Our loving King
  To you we bring
  Our praise!

Hosanna

Zechariah 7-9

Sing and rejoice, daughters of God!
    Shout for joy, sons of the Father!
Here comes your King
    travelling to his victory;
Riding humbly on a donkey,
    on a foal not ridden before.
Hosanna! All joy to our King!
    To the one who comes in the name of the Lord!

But my countrymen will not cheer;
    my people grumble at his coming.
Though their idols are useless,
    and their heroes are deceivers,
Though they wander like lost sheep
    without a loving shepherd,
Yet they will not listen,
    nor obey the word of the Lord.

He speaks up for true justice:
    'Give loyalty and compassion;
Care for the orphan and the pensioner;
    aid the refugee and those in poverty;
Do not ruthlessly exploit,
    or plot trouble for each other'.
But people will not listen;
    they shrug their shoulders and prepare a cross.

Ride on in majesty, King of love;
    show us the way that leads to peace.
The Lord shall banish our armies;
    our armaments shall be destroyed.
He shall speak reconciliation to every nation,
    extending his love from sea to sea.
This kingdom which seems impossible
    shall surely come to be.

Hosanna! Keep steady your hands!
    Hear the word of the Lord of hosts:
Love shall reign in the city of God,
    old people shall sit in its squares;
Its streets shall be filled with children
    playing without any fears.
The Lord will dwell with his people,
    and banish all sorrow and cares.

Forsaken?

My God! My God, why have you forsaken us —
forsaken us in the cry of the crucified?
In his horrible helplessness
we are doubly helpless,
suffering by the million
and dying
alone.

My God! The nails that pierced Jesus cruelly,
surely pierce our one humanity;
the taunts from bystanders are ours:
the secret doubt that all
ends in an empty whimper,
bereft of light and
love.

My God! That his life should thus mercilessly end,
surrounded by such malignant rejection,
loved only by a frightened few
watching in fear,
leaves us all in
dereliction and
despair.

My God! Into that cold stone tomb
fall all our noblest human dreams;
the idealism of youth sinks
low in the deep shadows,
and even desperate defiance
in the darkness
weeps.

Dear God! On that black Friday you did not forsake us!
Not Jesus, nor any other desolate child of man!
That day you entered all our forsakenness,
tasting bitter dereliction and death,
shaping the valley of the shadow
to become an avenue of
hope.

We praise you, O God! We acknowledge you to be the Lord!
Despised and rejected, man of sorrows and grief,
great and marvellous are your needs!
Wounded for our transgressions,
bruised for our iniquities,
God is with us!
Hallelujah!

The Suffering Servant

O Lord, our Lord,
we have heard the most unlikely story;
we have seen your saving power in a weak Man.

He grew up quietly like a lonely plant,
    rooted in arid ground.
There was nothing to make one notice him,
    no good looks to impress the crowd.
His people despised and rejected him;
    a suffering, pathetic, neglected creature,
from him most turned their faces,
    reckoning him as useless.

Yet, unlike anyone else, he bore our lot,
    and carried the full ballast of our sorrows;
but we carried on as if he deserved his fate,
    sentenced to misery by God.
The wounds he bore were for our faults,
    the crown he wore was for our violations;
He suffered shame to bring us peace,
    tasted pain that we might be healed.

We are as stupid as sheep,
     wandering and lost;
but in and through this Man
     you have carried our shame.
His rights were openly violated
     yet he took it without complaint —
like a ewe before drunk shearers,
     as a lamb led to slaughter.

From the land of the living he was cut off;
     by our sins he was struck down.
Though he was never a violent man,
     nor ever spoke a treacherous word,
he died between criminals,
     and was buried in a borrowed grave.

Yet You did not forsake this bruised servant;
     you made his death the unique death,
and did the most unexpected thing:
     He rose to life again!
After the agony came light;
     after disgrace came vindication:
victory for himself and for others,
     banishing the burdens of human disgrace.

Therefore this weak Man is for ever strong;
     His is the only, truly successful life.
He willingly staked his existence on you,
     and allowed himself to seem useless.
But, in fact, he bore our uselessness,
     and removed all charges against us.
His incomparable love-offering
     has become our true peace.

Good Friday

Lord, truly you have borne our griefs
    and carried our sorrows.
On this most terrible and wonderful day,
    when the sun was dimmed
    and the earth shuddered in horror,
We know it.

Lord, no longer is it only the blood of our brother
    that cries out from the ground.
Today we hear the voice of the blood of God
    pleading from the soil
    with a claim which will never be silenced
Or ever defeated.

Lord, everywhere we go your holy blood speaks:
    from the rocky soil of Israel,
From Australian wheatlands and the vineyards of the Rhine,
    out of the clays of Uganda,
    from the prairies of Canada and rice paddies of Vietnam:
The cry of love.

Lord, our homeland, too, shudders in loving recognition;
    everywhere is now Golgotha:
Aberdeen and Canterbury, Bodmin, Sunderland
    and Londonderry
    Cumbrian fells and South Downs,
Black Mountains and Norfolk Broads, all cry with the blood
    Of the crucified God.

Lord, if in love we offered you our homeland,
    it would be poor thanks;
If the whole wealth of Mother Earth were given,
    even that would be inadequate praise.
O you who bear our griefs and carry our sorrows,
We are yours!

Part Three

Astounding God

Astounding God

Astounding God!
Today I want to praise you
for amazing grace:

finding without seeking...
possessing without keeping...
the end where the beginning begins...
good news that is offensive...
doubting which is believing...
uselessness which is most useful...
the word that is speechless...
the death which dies...
poverty which owns the universe...
memory that looks forward...
emptiness which overflows...
bread which creates hunger...
mystery that is unmistakable...
the folly which is wisdom...
the Cross which is glory...
the God who is a servant.

For amazing grace
today I want to praise you!
Astounding God!

The Divine Secret
Ephesians 1

To the God and Father of our Lord Jesus Christ,
    Let our honour and praise be joyfully given!
In Christ the supreme blessings of eternity
    Are lavished on the children of time and dust!

Before the creation of the universe began,
    Before our planet received its shape and colour,
When tree had not yet grown nor bird sung,
    He planned us to be his special creatures,
To become complete without any flaw,
    Overflowing with the gift of love.

    Great and marvellous are your deeds,
        King of all ages!
    Beautiful are the works of your fingers,
        Lord of the beginning and the end!

It was his secret purpose and joy
    Through the power of the lovely Christ,
To destine us to become his own children,
    Releasing love and praise in all places.
For our liberation and fulfilment is certain
    Through the shedding of the blood of the Beloved.

    Wonderful is the name of Jesus Christ,
        Father of all mercy!
    Beautiful is the voice that brings our freedom,
        God of liberty!

Through the life of Jesus, freely offered,
    All our sins have been forgiven;
We see the wealth of amazing grace
    Poured upon us without limit,
Bringing a knowledge greater than all learning,
    And insight deeper than all sages and prophets.

    Who shall not marvel at your wisdom,
        God of our salvation!
    Who shall not tremble at the cost,
        Father of the Crucified!

The Divine secret, so long obscured,
    Prepared from the beginning in Christ,
Has now been shown openly to us,
    Implemented when the time was ripe:

Everything, absolutely everything in the universe,
    In the expanses of eternity and the confines of time,
Is to be brought into a glorious harmony
    Through the Christ, our incomparable Lord!

        Glorious is your secret,
            Reconciling God!
        Let prophets, apostles, and martyrs,
            And everything in earth and heaven,
        Exult with unbounded joy
            From generation to generation, evermore!

Easter

God of the risen Christ and our God,
we rejoice in your resurrection power,
which is fully ours in Jesus Christ,
and we pray that you will keep us alert
to the sufferings, needs, or duties
that burden many people this Easter.

Keep us prayerfully aware of those
from whom this Easter is one of misery and loneliness:
    those who are separated from loved ones,
    immigrants who are lonely in a strange environment,
    alcoholics and other addicts
    for whom no day is ever a holiday,
    homeless young people,
    unwanted old people,
    and the inmates of our prisons:
**Living Lord, help them to know your love in the message
    of Easter,
and to rejoice in the gift of the life in Christ.**

Keep us aware of those
for whom this Easter time is one of tragedy:
    especially the victims of road accidents,
    their family and friends,
    those who are seriously injured,
    those who are fighting for very life,
    and those who are weeping for the dead:
**Living Lord, help them to know your love in the message
    of Easter,
and to rejoice in the gift of life in Christ.**

Keep us aware, O God, also of those
who must work while most of
us are holidaying:
    **policemen and prison warders,
    transport workers, and entertainers,
    ministers and priests,
    ambulance men and nurses,
    cooks and nightwatchmen,
    and all those who are busier than usual
    in catering for guests:
Living Lord, help them to know your love in the message
    of Easter,
and to rejoice in the gift of life in Christ.**

God of Easter, keep each of us aware of our own needs,
and of the vast resources for our growth in faith, hope,
    and love,
which are available to us this day of resurrection:
through Jesus Christ our Lord.

Christ Is Risen

Christ is risen!
　　Christ is risen indeed!
Come you counties and boroughs, glorify the Lord!
　　From coast to coast, tell of his love!
Today all our defeats are defeated,
　　and death is swallowed up in victory!

Praise him, all you unemployed people,
　　your humiliation is not for ever!
Praise him, all unwashed and despised people,
　　your dejection shall be turned into joy!
Praise him, all prisoners in cells or in drug addiction,
　　your liberation begins at the empty tomb!
Praise him, all despairing and cynical people,
　　your fears are rolled away with the stone!
Praise him, all lonely and homesick migrants,
　　your risen Lord walks London streets, too!
Praise him, all who hurt from fresh bereavements,
　　your grief can be mingled with peace.
Praise him, all half-hearted Christians,
　　Your Lord makes all things new!

Christ is risen!
　　He is risen indeed!
With angels and archangels, and all the company of heaven,
　　let the people of our nation glorify his holy name!
Today all our defeats are defeated,
　　and death is swallowed up in victory!

Christians Together

Give praise to God who joins us here,
Whose healing Spirit casts out fear:
> Hallelujah, hallelujah!
Let each our neighbour's joy partake,
And to our God thanksgiving make.
> O praise him, O praise him,
> Hallelujah, hallelujah, hallelujah!

Give praise to God who gives us Christ,
Whose love redeems a mighty host:
> Hallelujah, hallelujah!
Let each our neighbour's faith uphold,
And to our God our joy be told.
> O praise him, O praise him,
> Hallelujah, hallelujah, hallelujah!

Give praise to God whose Spirit leads,
To serve mankind in all its needs:
> Hallelujah! hallelujah!
Let each our neighbour's hope repair,
And to our God all joy now share.
> O praise him, O praise him,
> Hallelujah, hallelujah, hallelujah!

This may be sung to the tune, Lasst uns erfreuen.

Trusting New Life

Spirit of new life,
grant unto us this day
   the grace to recognize new life
   breaking through
   in unlikely events;
and, in so recognizing it,
   to be ready to trust it
   and delight in it:
through Jesus Christ our Lord.

On the Rays of the Morning

God of the inner light,
come to us
   on the golden rays of the morning,
   warming moods that are frosty,
   enlightening minds that are gloomy;
and, as the sun swings higher,
so may our lives rise to you
   in the active praise of this day's duties:
through Jesus, our risen Light.

The Right-hand Man

God of the humble and homeless,
    the poor and the persecuted,
thank you for exalting Christ Jesus
    and giving him a name
above all other names.

Today we rejoice
that he who was the meekest and weakest
    of all earth's children
is at your right hand.

Now we know
that the homeless Son of man
    is more truly at home
than anyone else on earth.

Today we rejoice
that he who was the poor teacher,
    who begged for a cup of water,
    and slept on the wild heath,
shows us our way to glory.

With gratitude we sing
    of the Man on a cross
who's now the exalted First-born
    of a new, everlasting race.

God of the defeated and the lonely,
    the despised and the hungry,
the misjudged and the imprisoned,
    the suffering and the dying,
we rejoice with great joy,
    praising his name,
and adoring your love!

Our God

Your rainbow shines
  its hope across all lands:
Christ's new creation,
  grasped by loving hands.

You are the bridge
  which spans our separation;
Christ's life laid down
  the new foundation.

Your vast acceptance
  liberates from fear;
Christ's fellow-heirs
  high-spirited appear.

Full of surprises
  is Christ's God and ours;
the weak rejoice
  in unexpected powers.

Our roots grow deep,
  firm in the ground which holds us;
Christ's subtle strength
  where love enfolds us.

Jesus

Jesus, Son of Man,
    Jesus, Son of God,
radiance of the Father,
    first-born among many brothers:
to you belongs our sole allegiance
    and our everlasting gratitude!

When our world was ripe
    for despair of faith,
    you came to us.
With our uprooted hopes
lying fruitless around us,
    you shared our dust
    and planted a true vine
which shall ever be fruitful.

While proud and cultured men
    chased philosophical fashions,
    or created scribal absurdities,
You told unforgettable parables
    about farmers, servants, and wedding parties,
seeding the furrows of history
    with a potent Word bearing a harvest
    too vast for all the silos of this world.

In the terrible time of your dereliction,
when man attained his worst hour,
    you hung on that awful Cross
    bearing on tortured shoulders
    the sins of the whole world,
till in the gathering darkness
    you knew the task was done
    and the reconciliation begun.

In the light of Easter dawn,
    while disciples in whispers
    passed their despair one to another,
You arose at the call of the Father,
bringing light and immortality to light,
    warming hearts with inextinguishable joy,
    and rehabilitating doubters and deniers
with a love that overpowers the gates of hell.

Jesus, the Word made flesh,
    Jesus, friend of sinners,
Reconciler of the whole universe,
the resurrection and the life:
Heaven and earth are full of your glory!
Our allegiance and gratitude are yours for ever!

Reflection of the Unseen

Colossians 1

At the time when shadows were around us
and fears choked our joy,
You, most wonderful God, transferred us
into the kingdom of the Son of Love,
where there is the light
and liberty of the children of God.

Like the reflection of the sunrise
beaming over placid waters,
so is our Lord the true reflection
of you, our unseen God;
the beginning of all that was,
and the joyous completion
of all that is to be.

Our little planet
and the vast worlds in outer space
were spun by his power!
The things we see and discover,
and things no eye has seen
nor mind comprehended,
are all subject to his power
and filled with his purpose.

His ways are before all other.
The grace that coheres all things
is his and his alone.
The Church is his making
and he is its only head,
the first risen from all death,
the only Son to be named Lord.

Wonderful is your choice,
Most loving God,
to make the fullness of your nature
dwell in our True-Man Jesus,
reconciling the whole cosmos
to yourself through him,
bringing gracious peace
through the most bloody cross;
peace in time and eternity
through him alone.

Transforming Misfortunes

Most loving God,
in this cynical world help your people
to prove the hopefulness of existence
by turning negative situations into positive ones:
When we are weak, then we are strong.

Help folk to transform
disappointments into new courage,
or pain into greater caring and sharing:
When we are weak, then we are strong.

Help people to use sickness
for increased sensitivity toward all who suffer or grieve,
and to make us treasure our neighbours all the more:
When we are weak, then we are strong.

Help us all to use reproach for honest self-assessment,
and abuse for better understanding of others who are abused:
When we are weak, then we are strong.

Help the lost to use their dismay
to spur them into finding themselves and their true destiny:
When we are weak, then we are strong.

Help each of us here
to find your word though prayers seem unanswered,
and to hear your call in difficult opportunities:
**We can do all things through Christ
who strengthens us.**

Grace of Our Lord Jesus Christ

How shall we ever praise our Lord enough,
  Or serve him as he surely deserves?
His grace moves faster than light;
  His mercy is larger than the universe.

In every part of our home planet,
  Grace works without limit.
It saturates the weary centuries
  And fully fills each minute.

No nation is denied his grace
  Nor is any child outside it.
The cities and the farms partake alike;
  It works in lives that still deride it.

So deep that none can fall beneath it;
  In all the world no one is missed.
Our sins rise up, but ever higher
  His grace will rise and still persist.

What God's grace launched in Christ,
  Will one day be completed.
And though it suffer from a million blows,
  His grace will never be depleted.

Part Four

Life in the Spirit

Life in the Spirit

When earth was like a valley of skeletons,
    you, wonderful God, came among us in power!
Your Jesus breathed on us and said:
    'Receive the Holy Spirit'.
Like a mighty rushing wind:
    'Receive the Holy Spirit'.
Like tongues of living fire:
    'Receive the Holy Spirit'.
With love to the whole world:
    'Receive the Holy Spirit'.

Lord, if we had not seen and heard,
    we would not believe it;
That this valley of dry bones should live
    is beyond our wildest expectations!
Yet now we hear rattling of bones
    as dead and forgotten hopes reassemble;
We witness the astounding omen
    of broken, impotent promises growing muscle;
Surprised, we watch old eye-sockets
    filling with new and loving visions;
Cold arms pulse as with new blood,
    embracing lonely and uncherished people;
Deadly-dull churchgoers stand tall
    and celebrate the Gospel with style.
We see atrophied hands and feet inspired
    to do the costly deeds of Jesus;
Bare bones, bleached by the winds of materialism,
    become enfleshed with faith and love;
We hear voices, long ago incapable of blessing,
    commence to sing the songs of the angels.
Before our very eyes, unforgiving, bitter skeletons
    begin to be merciful, even as our Father is merciful;
Grey, defeated forms, who despaired of any joy,
    run and dance their way into the Kingdom!

Holy Spirit, Lord, and giver of life,
    praise belongs to you for ever!
The Gospel is announced to the poor:
    praise belongs to you for ever!
Release for prisoners, sight for the blind;
Yes, the time has come
    when the Lord will save his people:
    praise belongs to you for ever!

The Bountiful God
Psalm 104

With all my being I celebrate the Lord!
    My wonderful God, you are dressed in glorious love!
You come to us as bright as the sunlight,
    and signal to us out of the star-flecked sky.
You refresh us with rain and play on tumbling clouds,
    and ride on the wings of the wind.
The breezes are your messengers,
    and the sparkling fire is your servant.

In the first travail of our planet's birth,
    while earth's crust settled and seas found their shores,
While mountains stood tall and valleys nestled below,
    you were present with a word insistent as thunder.
You were the one who first poured streams down valleys,
    watching otter play and kingfisher dive.
You saw the nightingale arrive in our woodland,
    singing from among lush branches,
While the beech tree lifted high its head
    and the oak gave nesting place to magpie and owl.

Even now you are still at work;
    among the heather you shelter grouse and mountain hare.
The farmers look up as the clouds still give sweet rain,
    so that the grass grows and the sheep and cattle are fed.
Over fields of green corn the showers spread,
    and the thirsty hopfields are watered;
Across orchards and gardens sunshowers fall,
    till the face of man shines with happiness.

Your sun and moon revolve on,
   regulating all waking and sleeping;
After dark the wild creatures are on the move,
   then at dawn they slink back to their lairs.
In the rhythm of this good life man gets up to work;
   tired, he comes home at night and receives rest.

Lord, everything you do is so bountiful!
   The encircling sea swells with herring, cod and mackerel.
The world teems with living things, all depending on you,
   taking what you offer, feeding from your hands.
If you should hide your face, fear would overtake us;
   if you should withdraw your breath, all would be no more.
But you would only have to speak and all would be renewed;
   the face of the earth would be radiant again.

May your rule last for ever!
   May you always find joy in your precious planet!
We tremble with joy at your glance!
   We come to life at your touch!

Transfiguration Day

God of the transfigured Christ,
in your mercy transfigure us
and the whole world,
till the glory of Christ is seen
in the most unexpected places.

Transfigure our schools,
universities, medical schools,
and military colleges.

Transfigure our hospital wards,
our foster homes,
and our funeral parlours.

Transfigure our politics,
business and industry,
our laws and lawcourts.

Transfigure our friendships,
marriages, neighbourhood,
and all places of work.

Transfigure our charities,
overseas aid programmes,
our refugee procedures and hostels.

Transfigure the church universal,
the churches of...
and this congregation at...,
as we meet for worship and service.

And in your boundless grace, O God,
transfigure our own
personal faith, hope, and love.

Lord of the mountain and plain,
of vision and sacrifice,
let us live in the light
and glory of your love
today and for ever:
through Jesus Christ our Lord.

Holy Spirit, Help Us

Holy Spirit, you make all things new;
renew us in will and deed
to work together with you.

That all people, who today are shivering
with an icy loneliness at the core of their being,
may let go, and let God fill them with his warmth:
Spirit, hear us; Spirit, help us.

That Christians may be more willing to trust the Spirit
to fill and renew their lives and relationships:
Spirit, hear us; Spirit, help us.

That disabled people, the sick, and the disadvantaged
may find the Spirit with them and in them,
giving new courage and serenity:
Spirit, hear us; Spirit, help us.

That bitter people, disillusioned people,
and the angry ones who cause war or terrorism,
may find an inner healing of the Spirit
that will lead to peace and reconciliation:
Spirit, hear us; Spirit, help us.

That those who cause or tolerate injustice and inhumanity
may be brought to repentance
and find the way of the compassionate Spirit:
Spirit, hear us; Spirit, help us.

Spirit of God,
Gift of Pentecost,
remake us in the likeness of Christ,
that we may live to your glory,
from here to eternity.

City Pentecost

Through skyscraper canyons
    you come, Holy Spirit,
down lanes and arcades
    you come:
From the north, from the south,
from within and without,
    like wind
    like wind
the roar of Pure Wind,
you come
sweeping through
to renew.

In houses of parliament
    you come, Holy Spirit,
into lawmaker's chambers
    you come.
From above, from below,
from ally and foe,
    as truth
    as truth
the roar of Pure Truth
you come
sweeping through
to renew.

Through grand gothic arches
    you come, Holy Spirit,
to choir and high altar
    you come.
From the west, from the east,
from the font and the feast,
    like fire
    like fire
the roar of Pure Fire
you come
sweeping through
to renew.

Special People

We thank you, O God,
for those people who are channels of your love in our lives:
For those who gave us birth,
and, in the weakness of our infancy,
sheltered, nurtured, and treasured us.

For those who taught us to walk,
to talk and to explore tastes, smells, sounds,
and to experience the warmth
of belonging and embracing.

For those who overlooked our faults
and affirmed our strengths,
and the friends young and old
who share our tears and laughter.

We thank you, Lord,
for the people of strong faith
who stretch our minds and enlarge our capacity
to explore and understand your ways.

For those at every stage of our journey
who teach us trust by trusting us,
who enable us to love others
through the experience of being loved.

We thank you for those very sincere people
who have demonstrated the joys and disciplines
of the kingdom of God,
and especially people who taught us to love you,
rather than to be afraid of you.

God of love, God of Jesus,
for these healing experiences of growth and loving,
and for the knowledge that the best is yet to come,
we praise your holy name:
through Jesus Christ our Lord.

The Body
1 Corinthians 12

We are the Body of Christ,
    each one of us a limb or organ.
Let us glorify God in the use of our bodies,
    which is a most reasonable worship.

All who are Christ's hands —
    gifted in healing or helping,
    making music or machinery,
    painting, polishing or planting:
glorify God in your bodies.

All who are Christ's eyes —
    studying society and the Scriptures,
    noticing newcomer and nonentity,
    at microscopes, murals, and mathematics:
glorify God in your bodies.

All who are Christ's ears —
    aware of weeping and wandering,
    hearing harmony and hypocrisy,
    listening to laughter, logic and the lonely:
glorify God in your bodies.

You who are Christ's lips —
    teaching, training, testifying,
    singing, selling, satirizing,
    encouraging, enlightening, engendering:
glorify God in your bodies.

You who are Christ's feet —
    walking, working, waiting,
    striding into service and sacrifice,
    running to receive a prodigal:
glorify God in your bodies.

You who are Christ's heart —
    feeling the fellowship of faith,
    agonizing with drug addict and alcoholic,
    loving the least and the last:
glorify God in your bodies.

If one suffers, we all suffer;
   if one flourishes, we all rejoice.
We are the Body of Christ;
   let us glorify God in this holy Body.

Holiness

I saw the Lord
weeping
with Belfast widows
in sombre streets
where children learn little
except the shock
of sudden grief
or from their brothers
the way of hate
and toxic despair —
    weeping.

  Holy, holy, holy is the Lord of hosts;
  The whole earth is full of his glory.

I saw the Lord
gasping
for breath in those churches
wherever shallow worshippers
mouth blessing on the hungry
then drive home
to overfills of protein
and sport on the TV —
    gasping.

  Holy, holy, holy is the Lord of hosts;
  The whole earth is full of his glory.

I saw the Lord
hoping
in students scanning open books
roughly asking why
why
why

searching deep into friendly eyes
for seeds of truth
worth living for
and dying —
    hoping.

    Holy, holy, holy is the Lord of hosts;
    The whole earth is full of his glory.

I saw the Lord
agonizing
through corridors and chambers
of Westminster
where hollow men
salute expediency
consult the opinion polls
so that our future
will be the past repeated
spreading stench like the last —
    agonizing.

    Holy, holy, holy is the Lord of hosts;
    The whole earth is full of his glory.

I saw the Lord
angry
whenever church councils and committees
tardily
face agenda lifelessly
with no fire in the gut
no hope in the eye
no readiness to lose all
in the Kingdom which
comes first —
    angry.

    Holy, holy, holy is the Lord of hosts;
    The whole earth is full of his glory.

O Lamb of God, who takes away the sins of the world,
    Have mercy upon us.
O Lamb of God, who takes away the sins of the world,
    Have mercy upon us.
O Lamb of God, who takes away the sins of the world,
    Grant us your peace.

For Those who Hunger

God of Jesus, God of us all,
Only true and everlasting friend,
inspire us to pray and act with the compassion of Jesus Christ.

God, at this moment there are people who hunger for food,
    for a crust of bread, a piece of fish,
      or even the scraps in our garbage bins.
Please feed them:
Lord, hear our prayer, and make us your answer to prayer.

There are some people who hunger for liberty,
    to go as they please,
    to stay on at home or visit friends,
    to worship without hindrance,
    to vote for whom they please,
    to see the end of police, compounds, and prisons,
    to be reunited with those they love dearly.
Please give them liberty:
Lord, hear our prayer, and make us your answer to prayer.

And there are some who hunger to be useful,
    to share what wisdom they have learnt from life,
    to listen to a neighbour's worries,
    to work beside a weary friend,
    to be of use to their family, country or church —
    to be of use to you;
    but bad health,
    or shyness and timidity,
    or unsightly physical deformity,
    or the frailty of old age,
    or sorrow over old sins,
    holds them back and makes them useless.
Please show them how they can still be useful:
Lord, hear our prayer, and make us your answer to prayer.

Loving Father, there are some who hunger for your grace,
who look for faith,
who search for your meaning and your name,
who look for someone whom they can trust,
and hunger for something worth worshipping.
Please satisfy their hunger with the bread of life:
Lord, hear our prayer, and make us your answer to prayer.

And to you, dear Lord,
Father and Provider,
Christ and Saviour,
Holy Spirit and Friend,
be honour and glory,
worship and praise,
from now to eternity.

Hunger and Thirst

Unfathomable God,
you have given us hunger —
and the food to satisfy us,
the experience of thirst —
and the drink to quench it.
Can it be that,
hungering and thirsting for you,
we shall be denied satisfaction?

Water of life and Bread of Heaven,
give us stubbornness in our seeking,
persistence in our partaking,
honesty in our questioning,
so that we may not despair
nor abandon the effort to pray;
not chase attractive substitutes,
nor fail to listen
to your witnesses.

Help us to creatively meditate
on the wisdom of Scripture —
the ugliness of human sin
and the sadness of death,
the wonder of divine love
and the life of Christ —
until our inner lives expand
and we begin to understand.

O loving God,
the beyond who is among us,
the thirst and the quenching,
the hunger and the satisfaction,
help us to live out our own prayers,
trusting you more lovingly,
listening more carefully,
and obeying more faithfully.

Then will our thirsty desert
blossom like a rose;
in our wilderness
we will eat manna;
in our seeking
we shall be surely found.
The glory of the Lord shall possess us,
the splendour of our God be revealed,
and we shall truly rest.

For the Affluent
Psalm 49

Hear this, British Isles!
   Listen, all people on earth,
The teeming millions and every single person,
   the affluent and the needy!
For I have a sane word to speak,
   the truth from a full heart.

There are many who trust money,
   and show off their wealth.
Yet none can ransom themselves,
   nor bribe God for redemption.
To ransom their soul is far too costly,
   for ever beyond their means.

Remember: even smart people die;
   so, too, do the foolish and the callous.
All wealth is left for others;
   our home becomes the grave —
the place where we must remain
   though our name might linger on a business.

The privileged have no exemption;
   like animals we all perish.
Such is the destiny of fools,
   and of all who admire them.
Like sheep they flock to doom,
   with death their only shepherd.

Do not stand in awe of a rich man,
   who lives in an extravagant home.
He can take nothing with him when he dies;
   his vainglory shall not follow him.
But God shall ransom his humble people;
   he shall save us from the power of death.

Who Am I?

I am the joyful shepherds
    who heard the angels sing —
And the preoccupied innkeeper
    whose stable housed a King,

I am the three wise men
    who travelled from afar —
And the terrible King Herod
    who feared your rising star.

I am the disciples who followed
    the new friend they had found —
And the fussy scribes who found you
    uncomfortable to have around.

I am the prodigal son
    come home to my Father's place —
And the righteous elder brother
    who resented the gift of grace.

I am the rich man who lived it up,
    spurning the beggar at the gate —
And bustling, touchy Martha,
    who couldn't bear to sit and wait.

I am the crowd that gathered,
    wanting to put a crown on your head —
And I am the devil who tempted you
    with pleas for power, signs, and bread.

I am Zacchaeus who unprepared
    had you as guest and Saviour —
and the stiff-necked Pharisees
    who grumbled about your behaviour.

I am the crowd who cried 'Hosanna' —
    And Peter who let you down;
The police who did their duty well,
    and laughed at your thorny crown.

I am John who stood near your cross —
    And the soldiers who nailed the wood;
Mary who found an empty tomb —
    and Thomas, a risen Lord!

I am the apostles who took your Gospel
    to people everywhere.
Lord, I am just one hungry child
    with bread to eat and to share.

Touch and Heal Us

Most loving God,
    in whom we live and move
    and have our being,
give us new awareness of your presence.

Touch our minds,
    that we may know you
    in the word of Scripture
    and in the living Word, Jesus Christ.
Touch our ears,
    that we may hear you in music and song.
Touch our eyes,
    that we may remember you
    in the signs of cross and candlelight.
Touch our hearts,
    that we may love you
    with a love that sweeps through us
    like a great tide.

Living, loving Spirit of God,
touch us with the spirit
of love, joy, and praise.

Good to be Alive!

God, our Father in Christ,
it is good to be alive,
to share life with each other
in your wonderful creation:
**We are most grateful,
and we thank you, Lord.**

You have given us the opportunity
to see the spring flowers,
to watch trees in the wind,
to inhale the fragrance of the season,
and to feel the warmth of the air:
**We are most grateful,
and we thank you, Lord.**

God, it is good to rest in the evening,
and rise in the morning,
to walk upon this good earth,
to hear your whisper in many places,
and to sing your praise with many friends:
**We are most grateful,
and we thank you, Lord.**

Lord, like a generous friend
you share the whole world with us,
and you fill our cup to overflowing
with the wine of gladness:
**We are most grateful,
and we thank you, Lord.**

We want to sing, dance, and pray,
in gratitude for every good thing in your creation!
Especially we want to embrace and express your Spirit;
the Spirit that filled our Lord Jesus to overflowing,
the Spirit of mercy, forgiveness, courage, and new life;
the Spirit of love, and laughter, and peace:
**We are most grateful,
and we thank you, Lord.**

For your presence with us, around us, beneath us,
within us, behind us, and in front of us:
**we, your children, are most grateful,
and we thank you, through Jesus Christ our Lord.**

Save Your Children

God, most holy and most compassionate,
save your children from the evil
which lies in wait even for your saints.
God of great mercy, we pray
that you will forgive us for our addiction
to words instead of deeds:
Lord, hear us and help us.

That you will rescue us
from our suspicion toward those
who attend a different church,
speak with a different accent,
or vote for a different political party:
Lord, hear us and help us.

That you will make us alert
to the silences or the cries
of those who are too weak
to defend themselves against injustice:
Lord, hear us and help us.

Please awaken our sensitivity
to those hidden fears
and self-dislike
which may make some people so unlovely:
Lord, hear us and help us.

That we may face up
to whatever embarrassment,
apology, or restitution is needed
to right the wrongs we have committed:
Lord, hear us and help us.

That, by the grace, mercy, and peace
of our Lord Jesus Christ,
you will enable us to say goodbye
to old shame, pessimism, and fear,
and be glad to accept your free forgiveness:
Lord, hear us and help us.

Father of Jesus and our God,
in a world of mistrust and ingratitude,
anxiety and miserliness,
we give you thanks for your abundant generosity
and your loyalty towards us:
though our Saviour Christ Jesus.

Planting True Vines

Make our lives, good Lord,
through Jesus our true Vine,
living branches of faith, hope, and love
so that the existence of others may be enriched
and our own lives grow mature with the fruits of Jesus Christ.

For our brothers and sisters
in all their diverse needs,
we pray.

Where people have forgotten how to laugh,
touch them with your joy.
Where they have lost the art of mercy,
graft compassion and forgiveness within them.
Where they neglect to share bread, medicine,
trust and friendship,
stir new growth of love within them.

Lord,
our true Vine,
abide in us
that we may abide in you.

Let your presence support the weak,
encourage the sick,
comfort the dying,
guide the confused,
heal the broken-hearted,
soften the hard heart,
and sweeten the bitter spirit.

Let the harvest of our prayers,
be in your time
and in your way, most loving Lord.

The Still Centre

When we want healing at the core of being,
   we turn to you, God of Christ Jesus!
When we discover the still centre of the storm,
   it's you we find there, most wonderful Lord!

Sometimes our life seems a jumble of fragments;
   nothing matches nor fits together.
A feeling of being lost floods in like a tide;
   anxiety erodes our inmost selves.
We are permeated by seeping discomfort,
   as if we are at odds with our own soul.
All good humour hides itself away;
   peace and joy become mere memory.

Then it is we find it hard to care for others;
   we are too distracted to notice their needs.
Self-giving becomes an impossible calling;
   love shrinks into a four-letter word.
Even our capacity to listen closes down;
   our counsel is but jagged lumps of yesterday.

Father of Christ, we refind ourselves only in you;
    nowhere else do we find true integration.
At home with you we are at home with ourselves;
    in your love we begin to care for ourselves.
Your peace passes all understanding;
    your joy liberates the laughter within us.
We begin to hear, and care for others again;
    love is shared as from a depthless source.
How shall we thank you, most loving God?
    Can gratitude ever find adequate voice?
Still Centre of all the storms, we worship you!
    Crux of the universe, we glorify you!

God's Strength
Psalm 121

When I gaze at the ancient mountains,
    their huge strength steadies my trembling.
The strength of the Lord made the galaxies,
    and shaped this dear old planet.
You can never stumble out of his care;
    he who loves you never falls asleep.
The One who looks after you is awake,
    always alert to the cries of his children.
Your God cares for you,
    closer than your own right hand.
Even the fiery sun will not harm you,
    nor the barren face of the moon.
God will keep you going in hard times;
    he'll treasure your very being.
When you leave for work in the morning,
    and when you return home at evening,
He will surely be with you,
    this day and for ever.

Faith, Hope, and Love

Faith like a mustard seed,
Power so small:
Word growing into deed,
Reaching tall,
Gift for all.

Hope making all things new,
Vision grand:
Christ's dream which shall come true,
In our land,
Near at hand.

Love larger than the world,
Christ's new song:
Power from which death recoiled,
Love so strong,
We belong.

Faith, hope, and love are free,
Boundless store;
New heaven and earth shall be
Without flaw,
Evermore.

This may be sung to the opening horn call from Schubert's
Symphony in C, 'The Great'.

Enigma

God, the name above all other names,
sometimes I think my name is Enigma:
Made in your image,
but sculptured from dirt;
Possessing your breath,
    but inhaling with infected lungs;
Owning Jesus as my true Brother,
    but also related to Judas and Pilate;
As clear as moonlight over frosty paddocks,
    but as muddy as a buffalo's wallow.

Yet, on my best days,
when the air is clear
    and the sun is shining,
my spirit hovers like a lark
    between earth and sky,
singing the loveliest melodies
    I have learnt on earth,
longing, longing to unite them
    with the music of the heavens.

O God, because you truly love
this human enigma,
and made me a member
of your family,
let me learn some notes
    with which angels praise you,
and grant me the grace to echo them
    amid the mundane stuff of life.
For your love's sake.

Happiness
Psalm 1

Happiness is the person who shuns unloving ways,
　　who is not attracted by apathy or sarcasm,
But finds delight in Jesus' teaching,
　　testing it out by day and by night.

Such people are like willows
　　growing by the riverside.
Greening without fail each spring
　　and defying the heat of summer.

Not so unloving people;
　　they are like grass in stony fields.
They fail the testing of difficult days,
　　and are shamed in the presence of goodness.

Those who love have their tap-roots in God;
　　the unloving are rootless.
The Lord can work with loving people,
　　but the unloving work their own ruin.

Part Five

Never Alone

Such a Strange Mixture

I'm such a strange mixture, Lord;
something greater than human wisdom
    is needed to sort me out
    and make me whole.

Some days I soar like an eagle
    over the peaks of the Cairngorms;
Yet on other days I'm a cockroach
    hiding in dark places.

Sometimes, like a sailboard enthusiast,
    I truly enjoy riding life's rough waves;
But at other times I just sit and complain,
    allowing the waves to break over me,
    filling my eyes with grit
    and my soul with self-pity.

There are special moments of prayer
    when I beg you to take me hiking
    among the mountain-places of the Spirit—
Followed by pessimistic moods
    when my bleating prayers
    rise no higher than mole hills.

Lord, you have searched me and known me.
You know the strange mixture
    that hides behind my public face.
Take me in hand.
Be to me not the God I want,
    But the God I need.

When

Lord, when my prayers are like a lonely moor,
and my soul like a wintry fen,
warm me with the breath of your mercy.

When I take things for granted
and gratitude goes to sleep—
put a new song on my tongue
till I praise as naturally as the thrush.

When life' abrasive pressures fray me,
loosening my hold on the Still Centre—
tell me again about sparrows and ravens,
about bluebells, lilies and daffodils,
and the Father who knows my needs.

When my miserly soul begrudges love,
complaining about importunate people,
or hides smugly in the folds of apathy—
put into my hands a crown of thorns,
and show me again what love can make
of two pieces of wood and a few nails.

Familiar Things

Sing from the mountain-tops and shout to the skies!
   Praise him all his messengers, and cheer him all his servants!
Let all our Isles praise the Lord;
   mountain and fen, river, waterfall and farm.
Let the vegetation praise the Lord;
   oaktree and rhododendron, elm, bluebell and heather.
Let all animals praise the Lord,
   badger and rabbit, cattle, sheep and feral goat.
Let the birds of field and forest praise the Lord,
   pheasant and woodpigeon, cuckoo, woodpecker and skylark.
Let coastland and seas praise the Lord,
   surf and tides, sandhill, rockpool and starfish.
Let everything in the seas praise the Lord,
   mackerel and pilchard, halibut, seal and dolphin.
Let our cities take time to praise the Lord;
   park and street, housewife, dustman, and councillor.
Let all music praise the Lord;
   guitar and organ, orchestra, pop group and brass band.
Let everything living under the sun,
   everything that is or ever will be,
   praise the Lord! Hallelujah!

For Things That Go Well

In a world where many things go wrong,
   we praise you, God, for things that go well:
Marriages that are sound and beautiful,
   each person nurtured in respect and love.
Grandparents who share the make-believe of children,
   and grandchildren who love deeply in response.
Families where there is no generation-gap,
   where members can be together or apart without fuss.

We praise you for natural things taken for granted,
   the normal rhythm of continuing creation:
Trees that purify the polluted air,
   breathing in our waste and giving us oxygen.
The robust old sun that never rests,
   encouraging up from the earth our daily bread.
The never-failing power of water to quench our thirst —
   and a dozen tasty drinks dependent on it.

We praise you, God, for open spaces,
   where earth and its creatures can be enjoyed;
For the glory of beechwoods on Chilton Hills
   and golden eagles over Highland glens;
For the wooded islands of Windermere,
   and shaggy wild goats of Snowdonia.
For the blossom time in the vale of Evesham,
   and the hardy ponies roaming Dartmoor.

We praise you for folk who love their neighbours,
   genuinely looking for no reward.
For much-criticized churches which still keep going,
   treasuring the Gospel in spite of the cynics.
For the influence of that matchless Jesus,
   the best name in our prayers since childhood.
For the unearned times of courage, joy, love, and light,
   when your grace becomes our joy.

Exuberant Praise
Psalm 148

Cheer the Lord, everyone!
  Everything, praise him!

Cheer him from our skies;
  praise him from outer space.
Cheer him, you astronauts;
  praise him, all children of the stars.
Cheer him, sun and moon;
  praise him, all distant galaxies.
Cheer him, all who are close to his heart;
  praise him, all mysteries beyond our knowledge.
All of you, cheer the Lord,
  for he speaks and you come into being.
He gives you a place for ever;
  He fixes the universal laws.

Cheer the Lord from this planet earth;
  rolling ocean and powerful hurricane:
Lightning, hail, snow and ice;
  winds and storms fulfilling his purposes;
Our mountains, valleys and moors,
  our orchards, cornfields and forests;
Squirrel, hedgehog and fallow deer;
  puffin and falcon, robin and blackbird.

Prime ministers and presidents of the earth;
  Cabinet ministers and high court judges;
Exuberant teenagers,
  old people and children,
Come on, all of you, cheer the Lord;
  he alone is worth it!
His glory transfigures this earth,
  and blazes from a million suns.
He has given mankind high honour;
  heroes will applaud his faithfulness.
Those who trust his presence will shout:
  'Cheer the Lord!'

Morning Sunlight

As the morning sun falls on tiled roof-tops
 and spreads warmth in east west alleys,
My whole being rises to give praise;
 my every fibre rejoices in God.

Cars speeding on the motorway sparkle in light;
 in sunshine even the buses seem young again.
Already builders are at work on new houses,
 perched on rafters soaked with sunlight.
Laughing children skip their way to schoolgrounds,
 or pedal small bikes with spokes aflashing.
Across parks people short-cut to work —
 ladies stilt-stepping and men strong-striding.
Little children sun-dance to playschool,
 escorted by mothers, sisters, and brothers.
An old lady potters in her front garden;
 her husband promises the terrier a walk.
Overhead, gleaming planes jet interstate,
 while their teachers, the starlings, gather on power-lines.

Trains hoot through suburban crossings,
 and delivery vans begin their bustle.
Everything has wakened at the old sun's bidding;
 our whole city embraces a bright new day.

Blessed be your name, Giver of sunlight.
 Blessed be your name, Author of life.
Glory be to you, Lord of our city.
 Glory be to you, Renewer of life.

Daybreak

Most loving God,
we who worship in the early hours of this day
pray for the grace
to accept all duties and pleasures
as a gift from you,
and by the help of your Spirit
to allow all things
to work together for good:
through Jesus Christ our Lord.

This New Day

Most loving God,
you have given us this new day
in which to serve you
and to delight in you.

By your Spirit help us to do so,
not as slaves,
but as your precious children,
called to be the sisters and brothers
of our Lord Jesus Christ,
in whose name we gather this morning.

Shame and Glory

Most loving God,
we admit to you and to each other
that we are beings in whom shame and glory
are strangely mixed.
We are creatures of wisdom and folly,
   trust and anxiety, success and failure,
   truth and deceit, love and apathy.
We need you, yet we evade you —
   to believe, yet we doubt,
   to praise, yet dishonour,
   to love, yet resent.
God of the new creation and our God,
we wish to be made whole
   in thought, word, and deed.
We seek of you today the gifts of Jesus:
   forgiveness, renewal,
   self-acceptance, self-understanding,
and the courage to be
the sisters and brothers of Christ.

Faith

Living God,
   faith is your gift to us.
We thank you for the faith we have,
and pray you to enlarge it,
   so that, by faith,
   our hope in you will be more radiant,
   and our love purer, stronger,
   and more courageous:
through Jesus Christ our Lord.

Divine Generosity

Generous God,
Your open-handedness goes far beyond what we deserve,
and higher than our noblest aspirations.

We do not ask for more blessings,
but for the ability
to recognize, enjoy, and extol
the ones that are ours for the taking:
through Jesus Christ our Lord.

As Eagle and Dolphin

O God, you are my God:
early will I seek you,
my soul thirsts for you,
my flesh longs for you.
As the eagle belongs to the air,
and the dolphin belongs to the sea,
so we belong to you,
O God, my God.

The Word and the Babble

Loving God,
give us a lively and sensitive mind
that we may hear your Word
above the babble of human words;
and, so hearing,
may follow every suggestion
you make to us this day:
through Jesus Christ our Lord.

The Only Hope
Psalm 5

Lord, you hear what I'm saying;
   you see what I'm thinking.
My only hope is for you to keep listening;
   you're the only One to whom I can turn.
Every morning my tongue feels for the best words;
   when I wake up I want to praise you.
You don't find pleasure in our mistakes;
   for nothing unloving can live with you.
Stupidity cannot stand up to you;
   those who hurt others shall taste your displeasure.
For my part, I will come to church celebrating your love;
   in gratitude I'll turn my face to the Table and the Cross.
Lead me, Lord, in genuine goodness;
   show me the way which goes straight ahead.
Come, everyone who loves God, celebrate with me;
   join me in a shout of joy!
You care for them too;
   may they find utter happiness in you.
For you give happiness to all loving people;
   your caring love is stronger than steel.

Unspeakable Joys

Loving God,
you have knit together your people
in one communion and community
within the mystical body of Jesus Christ.
Give us grace
so to follow your saints
in all faithful living,
that we may participate in the unspeakable joys
which you have prepared for all who love you:
through Jesus Christ our Lord.

A Quiet Spirit

Teach us, good Lord,
to pray as we should,
so that we, who so often babble
like the heathen,
may be released from our much asking,
and brought to rest our lives
in the hands of the Father
who knows our needs before we ask him.

Dependable Word
Psalm 12

Help, Lord. What can we trust?
  Where is a dependable word?
Words no longer give communication,
  but are tuned for exploitation.
Men look us in the eye and lie;
  with secret motives they flatter us.
Lord, shut the lips of confidence men,
  and the tongues that exploit our pride.
Silence all media that twist the truth,
  the ad-men who can sell us destruction.

Listen! The Lord speaks,
  the only reliable voice is heard:
'Because of the plunder of the poor,
  and the groans of the lost,
I am among you, my people;
  I will protect you from the arrogant'.

This is the word we can trust,
  the pure word of Immanuel.
Like sterling silver is his word,
  refined seven times over.
He alone keeps his word,
  and saves us from the words around us.
Though scheming men oppose us,
  though voices cajole or bully us,
His word is the only word of life,
  the Word that endures for ever.

Hurry and Worry

God of eternity, creator of time,
giver of life and love,
rescue us from those pressures
which throw us off balance.

If today we have been in too much hurry
to realize that it is good to be alive:
Lord, have mercy.

If we live too close to the news headlines,
and not close enough to the eternal verities:
Christ, have mercy.

If we become so worried
that we forget that your grace is sufficient for us:
Lord, have mercy.

Timeless God, steadfast in love,
generous and patient with all your creatures:
**let the peace of our Lord, Jesus the Christ,
garrison our lives this day.**

Never Alone
Psalm 139

Lord, you see right through me,
    and know me utterly.
You understand what I'm thinking,
    long before I understand myself.
You are with me on the crowded street;
    beside me when I go alone to bed.
Everything I do, you recognize;
    my tongue never wags without you hearing.
I find you in my yesterdays and tomorrows,
    your love firmly around me.
All this is too much for me;
    It is beyond my understanding.

Where could I evade you?
    Where could I escape your presence?
If I live high with the jet-set, you are there.
    If I make my bed on a park bench, you are there.
If I could take off at the speed of light
    and travel the freeways of outer space,
Even there your hand would touch me,
    your right hand would hold me.
If I fear something awful will happen,
    like being swallowed by darkness,
My darkness will begin to shine like the day;
    for with you darkness becomes light.

How precious are your plans for me, Lord;
    they add up to a fantastic number.
If I tried to count them
    they would outnumber the sand.
Whenever I wake up to what's happening
    I find I'm still with you!
Lord, take a hard look at me;
    untangle my untidy motives.
Sort me out with your relentless mercy;
    weigh up all my ideas.
Tear away whatever is unloving in me,
    and lead me into your never-ending future.

Our Work

Lord, our attitude to work changes with our moods;
    we are as variable as the weather.
Some days we enjoy every moment of our work;
    other days we fill tired and resentful of it.
There are mornings when we dread the thought of getting up;
    but there are also times when we go to work gladly.

Lord, some of us get paid for doing the things we enjoy;
    others must work at distasteful tasks for their living.
Some of us work with kind and interesting people;
    others must work with sour and ugly characters.
Some who long for company must work alone;
    others who yearn for privacy must work with a crowd.

Lord, whether we work for love or pleasure,
    or whether it is only for duty or money,
We thank you for the privilege of daily work,
    for the rewards of labour in whatever form.
In a world where millions are unemployed,
    we count ourselves as richly blessed.

As products of the work of a loving Creator,
    we thank you for skills of eye, brain, and hand.
As friends of the carpenter's Son of Nazareth,
    we offer to you our work as an act of praise.
As children of the Spirit who has never ceased to work,
    we seek to honour you in everything we do.

Joys of Home Life

Let us praise the Lord for his goodness:

For our homes of the past and homes of today,
precious memories and present joys.
    Hallelujah, hallelujah!

For the intimate fun of family celebrations,
the enrichment of guests at our family meal.
    Hallelujah, hallelujah!

For the cries and cooing of a first baby,
the thrill of watching a child become adult.
    Hallelujah, hallelujah!

For little people chatting with make-believe presences,
and dolls, scooters, finger-painting, and birthdays.
    Hallelujah, hallelujah!

For pets that make our home their own —
dogs, guinea-pigs, cats, and budgies.
    Hallelujah, hallelujah!

For familiar walls holding out a storm,
and chairs and beds which have 'our feel' about them.
    Hallelujah, hallelujah!

For the shared excitement of planning new things,
and sorrowing together when things go wrong.
    Hallelujah, hallelujah!

For the love which allows us to be irritable with each other,
weakness accepted and strengths shared.
    Hallelujah, hallelujah!

For fragile ties which hold under strain,
forgiveness sought and forgiveness given.
    Hallelujah, hallelujah!

For our homes of today and homes yet to come,
present joys and hopes for tomorrow,
    Hallelujah, hallelujah, hallelujah!

Homes
Psalm 127

Unless home-life is built by the Lord,
  the carpenter's efforts are useless;
Unless a nation trusts in God,
  armies are quite worthless.
To work heavy overtime,
  or to run two jobs at once
in order to get rich quickly,
  is an exercise in futility.
For the Lord supplies our deepest needs,
  and his gifts are as free as sleep.

Children are a favour from the Lord,
  a family the loveliest reward.
Better than weapons to a soldier
  are children to godly parents;
They are indeed a happy couple
  who are hugged daily by tiny arms.
They shall never feel defeated
  when doubts and fears assail them.

Children in Hospital

Loving Lord, you know the joys and fears of little children.
Bless your little ones who are in hospital today:
If they are in pain,
give them the strength to bear it with your help.
If they are afraid,
give them the courage to share it with those who nurse them.
If they are so ill that only parents are allowed to visit,
help them to understand they have not been deserted
by sisters, brothers, or friends.

Gentle Lord, help the doctors and nurses
to be gentle, sensitive, and reassuring.
When painful treatment must be administered,
give your children confidence and trust in those who give it.

Put a sweet soothing prayer in the souls of the youngsters
who are too weak or too young to pray for themselves.
Above all else, help them to know they are never alone.
When family or friends leave and kiss them goodnight,
when the lights are turned low and quietness descends,
let them know for sure that you are at their side,
cradling them in strong warm arms,
soothing their fears and filling them with love and peace.

This is our prayer, through Jesus,
who shared our childhood and knows our pain.

Happy People
Psalm 128

Happy are those who honour God,
    sharing his ways.
You will work and eat;
    fun and goodness will be yours.
Wife and husband, like fruitful trees,
    shall tap the intimate joys of home.
Your children shall be like sturdy seedlings,
    growing straight and tall.
That's how it will happen
for those who honour God!
Happiness will come from his Church,
    and your worship will be a delight.
All the days of your life
    you will delight in his growing family.
Peace be to God's people!
    Peace be to his Church!

Good Shepherd

Most loving God,
in Jesus, who gave his life for the sheep,
you have opened up to us
the way of limitless life.

Help us to know Jesus our Good Shepherd,
   that we may be able to recognize his voice
   among the many voices that call to us;
and, knowing his voice,
may we have the courage
   to follow wherever he leads us,
that our lives may be opened
to the limitless life
which you offer to all your children.

This we pray,
in the name of our Good Shepherd,
Christ Jesus our Brother and Lord.

Thanksgiving for Light

Most wonderful God, we thank you for the gift of light:
For its power to cheer us, enliven us, encourage and guard us.
For the merry old sun, rising over our hills and calling us to
a new day:
**For moonlight and starlight, stirring a sense of wonder
and serenity within us.**

For street light, car light, traffic light, protecting
and guiding us:
For the beauty of city lights viewed from the hills.
For the beauty of affection lighting the faces of those
who love us:
**For the light of human compassion in hospital, nursing
homes, and counselling agencies.**

For the supreme light of divine love
in the face of the Man of Nazareth:
**For the radiance of Christ's goodness, grace and
self-sacrifice.**
For his light in his church, exposing, challenging, and
showing us the way to new creation:
**For his radiance in our individual lives, uncovering,
rebuking, forgiving, renewing, and guiding us.**
Most wonderful God, we praise you
for the Light of the world:
**Most merciful God, we praise you
for the Sun that is never eclipsed!
God of God, Light of Light,
Glory be to you now and for ever.**

Evening Prayer

The busy day now takes its rest,
as mother evening enfolds us in embrace.
The distant stars and galaxies signal
messages about a Creator so vast
that our minds stagger
and our hearts are filled
with loving awe.

O Lord, our Lord,
glorious is your name in all the universe.
What are earth's children
that you notice us?
And what is the mystery of divine grace
that you love us?
You give us faith to trust you,
even though we cannot see you.
You touch our minds with fingers of light,
and our hearts with forgiveness and peace.

As the evening moves on,
we go to rest
able to sleep the sleep of children
who know that, in life or death,
we are surrounded by love eternal.

O Lord, our Lord, glorious is your name
on earth and in the heavens!

Part Six

Come Quickly!

Father of the Lights

The Letter of James

Father of the lights of heaven,
God of the faith that works:
    Every good gift you present to us,
    unchanging legacies you give us.
    Not in passing moods
    but in calculated love
    you offer us a new vision
    through Jesus, Prince of light.

Father of the lights of heaven,
God of the faith that works:
    When our wisdom crumbles,
    you bring us true insight —
    uncomfortable yet comforting,
    costly yet absolutely free!
    Bonus-God, you never ignore
    or rebuff the child who asks.

Father of the lights of heaven,
God of the faith that works:
    Your brand of wisdom is practical,
    it is cheerful and merciful,
    rich in compassionate deeds
    and the foe of empty words.
    There is no longer room for blame,
    for the Lord is full of compassion.

Father of the lights of heaven,
God of the faith that works:
    Happy are those who remain true!
    Happy are the inheritors of your grace!
    They possess the promised gift,
    the large love of God,
    where widows and orphans are treasured
    more than crowns and fortunes!

The Ways of God
Psalm 19

The Signs of the Zodiac signal God's glory;
　　the Milky Way gleams with his handiwork.
Every new day tells his story;
　　at night-time his skills are displayed.
All nations and tongues can understand his language;
　　his message saturates our planet.
Look at the merry old sun in his robes of light;
　　he smiles like a bridegroom on his wedding day.
Keen as an athlete at the Olympics,
　　he strides from Tokyo to London.
Then he sprints the other half of the circuit,
　　missing no nation with his warmth.

How complete are the ways of the Lord,
　　constantly restoring our humanity.
He is a dependable counsellor,
　　with wisdom for those who have open minds.
The Lord's purposes are beautiful,
　　making our heart leap with joy.
His commands are clear,
　　bringing a new light into our eyes.
The respect he arouses is healthy,
　　extending for ever.
His assessment of us is fair,
　　completely to be trusted.
His word is more valuable than a fortune,
　　more precious than reserves of gold.
It is sweeter than the finest confectionery,
　　more natural than the comb of the honeybee.
It keeps your servants alert and sensitive;
　　living by it brings us incomparable gain.

If we should think he has made mistakes,
　　it's time to check our own motives.
Save your servants from self-conceit,
　　from the deadly reign of ego.
Then shall we live without shame,
　　free from the worst of all treason.
May these words tumbling from the mouth,
　　and the feelings surging in the heart,
Be acceptable in your eyes,
　　dear Lord, our true strength and our Saviour.

A New Song
Psalm 98

Come, sing a new song to God,
    for he has worked wonders!

With the strength of redeeming love
    he is saving creation.
He has brought his actions into the open,
    showing his love to all nations.
He has not forgotten his servants of old
    to whom he was so loyal;
But now every country on earth
    shall see what our God is doing.

Join the celebrations everyone,
    shout and sing for joy!
Praise God with the guitar;
    add your voice to the strings.
Join in with trumpet and drums
    till a joyful noise greets our King.
Let the sea roar and everything in it,
    the land and everything on it.
Come on, rivers, clap your hands,
    and you mountains, join the choir!

For the Lord comes to govern our planet,
    to deal out a new kind of justice,
And to make mercy his rule.

All Souls

Author of life abundant and eternal,
we thank you for the cloud of witnesses
    who make the mysterious heaven
    a home for our hearts.
Before you, we remember
    those faces we love
    and those spirits we treasure.

At radiant dawn
    and in the quiet of dusk:
we remember them.
Under summer skies
    with the farmlands shimmering:
we remember them.
Through winter's storms
    mid frost and snow:
we remember them.
At the return of spring
    with wattles clad in gold:
we remember them.
At birthdays and family celebrations,
    and in the festivals of the church:
we remember them.
When Christmas arrives
    with its carols and candles:
we remember them.
In the house of God
    as we sing and pray;
in the trumpets of the dawn
    on Easter Day;
in the Bread we break
and the Cup we take
    with eucharistic joy:
we remember them.

Come Quickly!
Psalm 63

My God in whom I trust,
　　I look for your early coming.
Body and soul, I thirst for you
　　like a man lost in the outback.
Through country and city I search for you,
　　looking for signs of your glory.
Your love is dearer than life itself;
　　my lips hunger for adequate praise.
As long as I live I'll serve you;
　　my hands shall honour your name.

When you come I shall be satisfied,
　　as a guest at a King's table.
I'll lie awake on my bed,
　　marvelling at your hospitality.
For you are my only help;
　　in your coming is true joy.
Willingly I'll be a disciple,
　　your strong hand pointing the way.

The false goals that distract me
　　shall crumble into the dust;
Everything that threatens my hope
　　shall be as carrion for the crows.
All deceit shall be silenced
　　when allegiance is sworn to you.
Let every ruler rejoice in you
　　when you come to be our King!

Judgment
Psalm 50

The only God has spoken;
   the Lord gives his word.
From beyond sunrise and sunset
   he calls the world to judgment;
From his city shines penetrating light,
   the radiance of sheer perfection.
Certainly he is coming,
   certainly he won't be silenced.
The fire of his presence will melt excuses;
   the wind of his spirit will break our defences.
Heaven and earth shall be summoned
   to the inescapable hour of reckoning.
Even his faithful friends must come,
   and the people of his covenant.
The skies shall ring with judgment
   when God delivers his verdict.

God's word is plain for the hypocrite;
   his grounds are completely clear:
'How dare you quote texts,
   you who evade renewal!
How can you glibly mouth my words,
   you who turn your backs?
You approve society's lawful thieves;
   you share in love's devaluation.
You are stuffed to the teeth with evil;
   your tongue frames smooth lies.
Every day you hound your brothers
   and stab your sisters in the back.
This and far worse you have done.
   Should I now keep quiet?
You even try to mould me in your own image!
   Openly shall I discipline you!'

Think about it,
   you who forget your God.
If the Lord tears your defences to pieces,
   who is there to save you?

But those who gladly give him all
   shall know a glorious freedom!
Those who worship in word and deed
   will see the salvation of God!

Endless Love

We thank you, God,
through our Lord Jesus Christ,
for the assurance of forgiveness
and the promise of renewal.
Your everlasting name
is mercy and love.
At morning, noon, and night,
You are mercy and love.

You are compassion;
Your love never ends.
You are our hope;
Your love never ends.
You are our inspiration;
Your love never ends.
You are true liberty;
Your love never ends.
You are joy and peace;
Your love never ends.

At morning, noon, and night,
you are mercy and love.
Holy is your name
above all names;
and, by your grace,
holy is our gratitude:
**through Jesus Christ,
our Saviour and our Brother.**

His Arms

Lord, your arms reached out
    to save a vagrant world:
    baby arms, embracing mother and father;
    boyish hands, holding a sacred scroll;
    brotherly arms, helping family and friends.

Lord, your arms reached out
    to signal a new beginning:
    acknowledging the Baptist at the Jordan,
    beckoning to fishermen by the sea,
    pointing to the narrow way that leads to life.

Lord, your arms reached out
    to stop the pain around you:
    straightening curved spine and crippled leg,
    opening the eyes of the blind,
    touching the skin of the lonely leper.

Lord, your arms reached out
    to welcome those who despised themselves:
    sharing bread with outcasts,
    writing in the dust for a broken woman,
    shaking the hand of Zacchaeus.

Lord, your arms reached out
    to express the divine anger:
    pushing Peter out of your way,
    shaking a fist at arrogant Pharisees,
    cleansing the temple with a whip.

Lord, your arms reached out
    to bear the burden of man's sin:
    washing the feet of fickle disciples,
    carrying a cross through jeering crowds,
    embracing the world with crucified arms.

Lord, your arms reached out
    to break the bonds of awful death:
    greeting the astounded disciples,
    showing Thomas the wounds of love,
    sending your witnesses to the ends of the earth.

Lord, your arms reach out
   transcending time and space:
   beckoning us to turn and follow,
   serving us the bread and wine,
   touching us with renewing grace.

Lord, your hands shall reach out
   gathering folk from every nation:
   breaking down walls that divide us,
   reconciling humanity through your cross,
   handing to the Father the finished new creation!